More Reasons for Reading

M000218382

Carrie Dobbs
William Rainey Harper College

Frank Dobbs
Northeastern Illinois University

Prentice Hall Regents
Englewood Cliffs, NJ 07632

Library of Congress Cataloging-in-Publication Data

Dobbs, Carrie.
    More reasons for reading / Carrie Dobbs, Frank Dobbs,
      p.   cm.
    ISBN 0-13-594433-3
    1. English language—Textbooks for foreign speakers. 2. Reading
(Higher education) 3. College readers. I. Dobbs, Frank.
II. Title.
PE1128.D54 1992
428.6'4—dc20

                                91-41208
                                CIP

Acquisitions Editor: Anne Riddick
Editorial Production/Supervision
  and Interior Design: Rachel J. Witty, Letter Perfect, Inc.
Cover Design: Carol Ceraldi
Photo Researcher: Rhoda Sidney
Copy Editor: Adele Gorelick
Prepress Buyer: Ray Keating
Manufacturing Buyer: Lori Bulwin
Scheduler: Leslie Coward

© 1992 by Prentice-Hall, Inc.
A Simon & Schuster Company
Englewood Cliffs, New Jersey 07632

Printed in the United States of America
10 9 8 7 6 5 4 3 2 1

ISBN 0-13-594433-3

*To
Cassie,
Frank C.,
and Seth*

Prentice-Hall International (UK) Limited, *London*
Prentice-Hall of Australia Pty. Limited, *Sydney*
Prentice-Hall Canada Inc., *Toronto*
Prentice-Hall Hispanoamericana, S.A., *Mexico*
Prentice-Hall of India Private Limited, *New Delhi*
Prentice-Hall of Japan, Inc., *Tokyo*
Simon & Schuster Asia Pte. Ltd., *Singapore*
Editora Prentice-Hall do Brasil, Ltda., *Rio de Janeiro*

CONTENTS

Chapter 8
FILLIAL PIETY OR REVERENCE FOR PARENTS *142*

Chapter 9
LAW AND ORDER   *160*

UNIT 4   ASTRONOMY
Chapter 10
THE SPEAR AT THE EDGE OF THE UNIVERSE   *180*

Chapter 15
FYODOR DOSTOEVSKY   *276*

PREFACE

This text is designed for the low-intermediate to intermediate pre-college/ university ESL student. It is designed primarily for close reading in-class work. The exercises are intended to help students comprehend the specific reading selection while learning skills that will help them comprehend future readings.

Students at this level need to expand their vocabulary, so the vocabulary exercises are quite extensive. Vocabulary is taught in context and is recycled consistently throughout the reading selections. In addition, these students need to be exposed to somewhat more complex syntax, so the skill exercises are designed to help them in this area and with recognition of topics, details, and organization.

The writing assignments are designed to encourage the students to interact with the readings or to react to them, using personal experience.

The reading selections are content oriented and include the areas of cultural anthropology, the human brain, non-Western ideas, astronomy, and biographies. There are three chapters in each unit, so that students read in depth on a wide variety of topics.

I usually read the reading selections aloud, while the students follow in their books. This helps the students complete the first reading of the selection without stopping to use their dictionaries. Reading aloud also helps the students with pronunciation of individual words that the sound systems of their own languages may cause them to misread—for example, *right* for *light, cloud* for *crowd, green* for *grin,* and so forth. Reading aloud to the students also allows them to hear intonation and juncture of parts of sentences and between sentences. In addition, reading aloud reinforces the connection between the written and spoken words, and can aid those whose learning abilities are more aural than visual.

Scanning exercises and vocabulary exercises should be completed without using dictionaries. After reviewing these exercises, I feel that some students will learn more, if they use their dictionaries. This is debatable, I realize, but different students learn differently, and it has been my experience that some students benefit from the use of dictionaries at certain times.

Field testing has indicated that the pre-reading discussions are most helpful and productive if done in small groups. There are also suggestions for other exercises which can be done in small groups or in pairs.

ACKNOWLEDGMENTS

Many thanks go to the students who tested the material and offered helpful comments—both as to what they liked and what needed changing. Special thanks go to Nicole Vonwyl, a student from Switzerland, who read the Reading Selections for their interest value.

Much appreciation also goes to Arlene Bublick for her help in field testing the material. To friends and colleagues Wally Sloat, Carol Piotrowski, and Arlene Bublick go thanks for reading and commenting on the material, as well as for their continued support.

Our production editor, Rachel J. Witty, has contributed many good ideas, and it has been a pleasure to work with her. Last, but certainly not least, we want to thank our editor, Anne Riddick, for her support and professionalism.

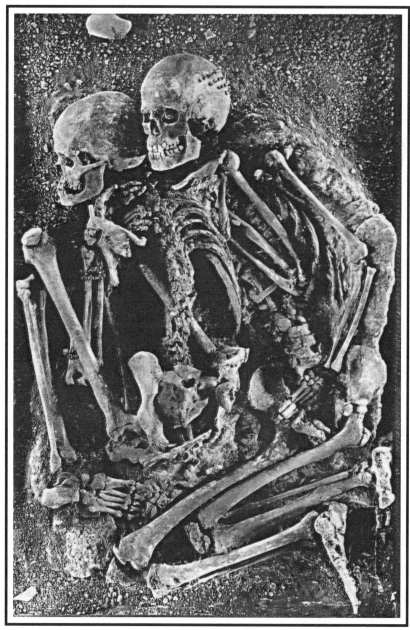

Ancient burial sites often provide clues to cultural beliefs and practices.
Courtesy of the American Museum of Natural History.

1 What Is Culture?

In small groups, discuss the following questions. When the discussions are finished, the groups can share their answers with the rest of the class.

- What does the word "culture" mean to you?
- Where do people get married in your country?
- What do you wear to get married?
- Do you have a party after you get married? What is it like?
- Are there cultures where it is legal for a man to have more than one wife?
- Is there any place where it is legal for a woman to have more than one husband?
- Do you think it would be good to have more than one wife or husband? Why? Why not?
- What are the most popular foods in your country?
- What do you like most to eat?
- What are some things that you don't like to eat?
- Do you think that red hair is beautiful? Black hair?
- Would you like someone who had green hair?
- When people die, what are the customs in your country?
- Do other people have different customs for this?
- Are other people's customs good or bad?

What Is Culture?

The word *culture* has many different meanings. For example, we sometimes say that people who know about art, music, and literature are cultured. However, the word *culture* has a different meaning for anthropologists (people who study humankind). To an anthropologist the word *culture* means all the ways in which a group of people act, dress, think, and feel. People have to learn the cultural ways of their community; they are not something that the people in the group are born with.

(2)   Instinctive behavior, on the other hand, is a pattern of behavior that an animal is born with. Spiders spinning their webs are examples of instinctive behavior. The mother spider does not teach her babies how to spin webs. (In fact, she is not even there when they are born.) They know how to do it when they are born. This is what we mean by instinctive behavior. Baby birds will instinctively run away if a cardboard shape of a hawk is moved forwards over their heads. However, they do not run if the cardboard shape is moved backwards. Hawks do not fly backwards, so the baby birds' instinct does not tell them that there is any danger. Their instinct is quite specific: The shape of the hawk must be moving in the correct direction.

(3)   As humans, we learn some of the ways of our culture by being taught by our teachers or parents. We learn more of the ways of our culture by growing up in it. We see how other people in our culture do things, and we do them the same way. We even learn how to think and feel in this way.

(4)   All human beings have certain basic needs, such as eating, drinking, keeping warm and dry, and so on. However, the way in which they take care of these needs depends on the culture in which they grow up. All cultures have ways of eating, drinking, dressing, finding shelter, marrying, and dealing with death. The foods that we think are good to eat, the kinds of clothes we wear, and how many people we can marry at one time are all parts of our culture.

(5)   Our own culture seems very natural to us. We feel in our hearts that the way that we do things is the only right way to do them. Other people's cultures often make us laugh or feel disgusted or shocked. We may laugh at clothing that seems ridiculous to us. Many people think that eating octopus or a juicy red piece of roast beef is disgusting. The idea that a

man can have more than one wife or that brothers and sisters can marry each other may shock other cultures.

(6)   Ideas of what is beautiful differ from one culture to another. The Flathead Indians of North America used to bind the heads of babies between boards so they would have long sloping foreheads. In the Flathead culture, long sloping foreheads were beautiful. Other cultures might think that they are strange-looking and unattractive. A tribe of Peruvian Indians shaped their children's skulls into tall, narrow, domes. The Chinese used to bind women's feet because they regarded small feet as beautiful. (These small feet were also a sign that the husband was wealthy. Because the women could not walk very well, they could not do much housework, and so the small feet showed that the husband could afford to have many servants.) Many people cut scars into their bodies or tattoo themselves so that others in their culture will think they are beautiful. Objects are inserted in holes in the nose, lips, and ears in a number of different cultures. In many twentieth-century societies, rouge, lipstick, eye shadow, perfume, and hair spray are all used to increase attractiveness.

(7)   When people die, different cultures dispose of their bodies in different ways. Sometimes bodies are burned. Sometimes bodies are buried in the ground. In many cultures in the past, people were buried with food, weapons, jewelry, and other things that might be useful in the next life. For example, the ancient Egyptians buried people with little human figures made from clay. These clay figures were supposed to work for the dead person in the other world. A religious group called the Parsees exposed their dead on platforms for birds to eat. Some people practice a second burial. After the bodies have been in the earth for several years, the bones are dug up and reburied, sometimes in a smaller container.

(8)   These are just a few of the many different customs that are found in different cultures. Most of the time, the different ways that are the customs of different cultures are neither right nor wrong. It is simply that different people do the same things in different ways.

EXERCISES

Scanning Questions

Look back at the reading selection for the answers to the following questions. Each answer is part of a sentence in the reading. Do not write the whole sentence. Write only the part that is asked for.

▐▶ *Example*

What has many different meanings? _____

Look for the words "different meanings" in paragraph 1. The sentence with the words "different meanings" is

The word *culture* has many different meanings.

The answer to the Example question is: The word *culture*

Do not read every word. Look quickly through (scan) each paragraph and look for key words, as in the example above.

Paragraph 1

1. What are anthropologists?

   _____

2. To an anthropologist, what does the word *culture* mean?

   _____

3. Do people know the ways of their culture when they are born, or do they have to learn these ways?

   _____

Paragraph 2

4. What is instinctive behavior?

   _____

5. What are examples of instinctive behavior?

   _____

Paragraph 3

6. How do we learn some of the ways of our culture?

   _____

7. How do we learn more of the ways of our culture?

   _____

Paragraph 4

8. What are some basic needs that human beings have?

   _____

9. What does the way in which human beings take care of their needs depend on?

   _____

Paragraph 5

10. What do we feel in our hearts is the only way to do things?

    _____

11. What often make us laugh or feel disgusted or shocked?

    _____

Paragraph 6

12. What differs from one culture to another?

_____

13. In the Flathead culture, what were beautiful?

_____

14. What did the Chinese used to regard as beautiful?

_____

15. Why do many people cut scars into their bodies or tattoo themselves?

_____

Paragraph 7

16. What are two different ways in which cultures dispose of bodies?

_____

17. What did the ancient Egyptians bury people with that were supposed to work for them in the other world?

_____

Vocabulary

Below are a list of vocabulary words and 7 pairs of sentences. Sentence **a** of each pair is from the reading selection. Look back in the reading selection and find the correct vocabulary word for sentence **a**.

Next, read sentence **b** carefully. On the blank line in sentence **b**, write the same word that you used in sentence **a**.

▸ *Example*

(From the first sentence of Paragraph 1)

    a. The word *culture* has many _____ meanings.

    b. An apple is _____ from an orange.

Sentence **b** of each pair uses the same word as sentence **a** with the same meaning.

basic	depends	pattern	specific
behavior	natural	shape	

1a. Spiders spinning their webs are examples of instinctive

    _____.

   b. Some children cry when they see a big dog. Other children show a

    different _____ when they see a dog. They smile at the dog.

2a. Instinctive behavior is a _____ of behavior that an animal is born with.

   b. My friend wakes up at 6:30 every morning, runs for two miles, and

    eats breakfast at 8:00. This _____ never changes. He does the same thing every morning.

3a. Baby birds will instinctively run away if a cardboard

_____ of a hawk is moved forwards over their heads.

b. ○ ← This _____ is a circle.

△ ← This _____ is a triangle.

4a. Their instinct is quite _____.

b. My friend asked me to buy her a blouse. She was very

_____ about the blouse. She wanted a short-sleeved light blue cotton blouse with white buttons.

5a. All human beings have certain _____ needs.

b. The _____ operations of arithmetic are addition, subtraction, multiplication, and division.

6a. However, the way in which they take care of these needs

_____ on the culture in which they grow up.

b. Her eyes look blue when she wears a blue sweater. Her eyes look green when she wears a green sweater. The color of her eyes

_____ on the color of her clothes.

7a. Our own culture seems very _____ to us.

b. It is not _____ for human beings to walk on their hands.

Do the same with the following:

afford	dispose (of)	increase	unattractive
container	expose(d)	regard(ed)	

8a. Other cultures might think that they are strange-looking and

_____.

b. Some people think that red hair is pretty. Other people do not like

red hair. They think that red hair is _____.

9a. The Chinese used to bind women's feet because they

_____ small feet as beautiful.

b. Some people _____ rock music as great music. Other people think that rock music is bad.

10a. Because the women could not walk very well, they could not do much housework, and so the small feet showed that the husband

could _____ to have many servants.

b. I can't _____ to buy a new car. It costs too much. I am going to buy a used car.

11a. In many twentieth-century societies, rouge, lipstick, eye shadow,

perfume, and hair spray are all used to _____ attractiveness.

b. I like very sweet cookies, so I usually _____ the amount of sugar in the recipe. When I use more sugar, I like the cookies better.

12a. When people die, different cultures _____ of their bodies in different ways.

b. We don't keep garbage in the house. We _____ of it. We put it in garbage cans outside, and the garbage collectors take it.

13a. A religious group called the Parsees _____ their dead on platforms for birds to eat.

b. Some people think that tan bodies are beautiful, so they

_____ themselves to the sun.

14a. After the bodies have been in the earth for several years, the bones are dug up and reburied, sometimes in a smaller _____.

b. The gas tank of a car is the _____ for its gasoline.

Self-Test

Fill in the correct words from the list below. Compare your answers with a classmate.

afford	container	exposed	pattern	specific
basic	depends	increase	regard	unattractive
behavior	dispose (of)	natural	shape	

1. Mary is usually a happy, smiling little girl. But when she is sick, her

   _____ is different. She is unhappy and cries a lot.

2. John gets up every weekday morning at 7:00, eats breakfast, and

   goes to work at 8:30. But on weekends, this _____
   changes. He sleeps until noon, and he doesn't eat breakfast.

3. A ball has a round _____.

4. Food is a _____ necessity for human beings. Without
   food, humans will die.

5. Our writing instructor was very _____. She told us to
   use 8 1/2″ by 11″ white lined notebook paper for our writing.

6. Breathing is _____. It is not something that we have to
   learn to do.

7. Mary liked her new dress. She thought that it was very pretty. Her
   friends did not like it. They thought that she looked

   _____ in it.

8. We are planning to have a picnic tomorrow, but it

   _____ on the weather. If it rains tomorrow, we can't have a picnic.

9. A bottle is a good _____ for milk.

10. Mary grew three inches last year. Because of the _____ in her height, her clothes were all too small for her.

11. Paper handkerchiefs (facial tissues) are easy to _____ of. We just throw them in a waste basket.

12. Private universities in the United States are very expensive. Many

    parents cannot _____ to send their children to private universities.

13. Some people eat insects. Other people do not _____ insects as food.

14. Flowers must be _____ to light. If flowers do not get light, they will not grow.

Pronoun Reference/Substitution

The following words are pronouns:

I	we	me	us	my/mine	our/ours
you				your/yours	
he		him		his/his	
she	they	her	them	her/hers	their/theirs
it				its/its	
this	these				
that	those				

Note: **my, your, his, her, its, our,** and **their** are called possessive adjectives because they modify nouns.

Pronouns can take the place of (substitute for) other words. Sometimes a pronoun substitutes for a single noun. The noun comes first:

    a. **Bob** was tired.
    b. **He** went home.

We say that **He** in sentence **b** refers to **Bob** in sentence **a**.
Pronouns can also substitute for a group of words:

    a. **My neighbor's dog** is brown.
    b. **It** barks a lot.

It in sentence **b** refers to **My neighbor's dog** in sentence **a**.
Sometimes a pronoun refers to a whole sentence:

    a. **Mary was sick yesterday.**
    b. **That** is why she stayed home.

That in sentence b substitutes for **all of sentence a**.

Below are sentences from the reading selection ''What Is Culture?'' Read the sentences and answer the questions.

  1. People have to learn the cultural ways of their community; they are not something that the people in the group are born with.

    What is the first pronoun? _____

    What does it refer to? _____

    What is the second pronoun? _____

    What are not something that the people in the group are born with?

    _____

  2. The mother spider does not teach her babies how to spin webs. They know how to do it when they are born.

    In the second sentence, what is the first pronoun? _____

    What does the pronoun refer to? _____

What is the second pronoun? _____

What do baby spiders know how to do when they are born?

_____

3. Baby birds will instinctively run away if a cardboard shape of a hawk is moved forwards over their heads. However, they do not run if the cardboard shape is moved backwards.

   What is the pronoun in the second sentence? _____

   What does the pronoun refer to? _____

4. Hawks do not fly backwards, so the baby birds' instinct does not tell them that there is any danger.

   What is the pronoun in the above sentence? _____

   What does it refer to? _____

5. We learn more of the ways of our culture by growing up in it.

   What do we grow up in? _____

6. All human beings have certain basic needs such as eating, drinking, keeping warm and dry, and so on. However, the way in which they take care of these needs depends on the culture in which they grow up.

   What does "they" refer to? _____

   What are "these needs"? _____

7. The Flathead Indians of North America used to bind the heads of babies between boards so they would have long sloping foreheads.

   What does the pronoun "they" refer to? _____

8. In the Flathead culture, long sloping foreheads were beautiful. Other cultures think that they are strange-looking and unattractive.

   What do other cultures think are strange-looking and unattractive?

   _____

9. The Chinese used to bind women's feet because they regarded small feet as beautiful.

   Who regarded small feet as beautiful? _____

Organization: Main Topics and Details

Paragraphs 5, 6, and 7 are organized in a similar way. First, there is a general statement of the main topic of each paragraph. Then there are specific examples of the information in the general statement. Sometimes there are also some extra details about each example.

Look at paragraph 5. The general statement of the main topic is

Other people's cultures often make us laugh or feel disgusted or shocked.

The examples are:

laugh	We may laugh at clothing that seems ridiculous to us.
disgusted	To many people, the thought of people eating octopus or a juicy red piece of roast beef is disgusting.
shocked	The idea that a man can have more than one wife or that brothers and sisters can marry may shock other cultures.

Look at paragraph 6.

There are six examples of things that different cultures think are beautiful. The first one is

Example: **In Flathead culture, long sloping foreheads were beautiful.**

Detail: How did they get long sloping foreheads?

_____

Example: What did the Chinese regard as beautiful?

_____

Detail: How did they make the women's feet small?

_____

Examples: What do some other cultures think is beautiful?

_____   _____

_____   _____

Look at paragraph 7.

What is the general statement of the topic?

_____

There are four specific examples of the ways that different cultures dispose of their dead. What are they?

Examples:

_____   _____

_____   _____

Details: What did some people bury their dead with?

_____

_____

Comprehension Questions

Answer the following questions by circling **True** or **False** for each statement. If a statement is false, explain why it is false. Write the statement correctly. Look back at the reading if necessary.

Paragraph 1

1. **True** or **False**   The word *culture* has more than one meaning.

2. **True** or **False**   People learn the way that they act, dress, think, and feel.

Paragraph 2

3. **True** or **False**   Instinctive behavior is learned.

4. **True** or **False**   The baby birds' instinct about hawks is specific.

Paragraph 4

5. **True** or **False**   People in all cultures have the same basic needs.

6. **True** or **False**   All cultures take care of these needs in the same way.

Paragraph 5

7. **True** or **False**   People in some cultures eat octopus.

8. **True** or **False**   A man may have more than one wife in some cultures.

Paragraph 6

9. **True** or **False**   Everyone has the same idea of what is beautiful.

Paragraph 7

10. True or False   The ancient Egyptians believed that a dead person went to another world.

Paragraph 8

11. True or False   Most of other people's customs are bad.

✑ Writing Assignment

Discuss the following questions with a partner:

What are your ideas of beauty?
How would you describe a beautiful woman?
What would a handsome man look like?

When you finish your discussion, write a description of a beautiful woman and a handsome man. Use your dictionary to find the words that you want to use.

Americans love tomatoes best, even though other vegetables are
more nutritious. *Courtesy of Ball Brothers Company.*

2

Food and Culture

PRE-READING DISCUSSION

In small groups, discuss the following questions.

- What are some foods that you will not eat? Why won't you eat them?
- Could you eat a butterfly? If not, why not?
- How would you feel if you saw someone else eat a butterfly?
- Do you think that what you eat is part of your culture?
- Why don't all cultures like and dislike the same foods?
- Have you ever heard the word "taboo"? For example, in many cultures, brothers and sisters are not allowed to marry each other. It is taboo to do so.
- Can you think of any other taboos?
- Why are some foods taboo in some cultures?
- Are pets (dogs, cats, birds) important to people in your culture?
- How do you feel about pets?

READING SELECTION

Food and Culture

W e all have ideas about what kinds of foods are good to eat. We also have ideas about what kinds of food are bad to eat. As a result, people from one culture often think the foods that people from another culture eat are disgusting or nauseating. When the famous boxer Muhammad Ali visited Africa, for example, one member of his group became quite sick when he saw someone pick up a butterfly and eat it. Many people would find it disgusting to eat rats, but there are forty-two different cultures whose people regard rats as appropriate food.

(2)   Some people in Africa think African termites make a delicious meal. Many other people would probably be sick if they had to eat termites, but one hundred grams of termites contain more than twice as many calories and almost twice as much protein as one hundred grams of cooked hamburger.

(3)   However, food likes and dislikes do not always seem related to nutrition. For example, broccoli is first on a list of the most nutritious common vegetables, but it is twenty-first on a list of vegetables that Americans like most to eat. Tomatoes are sixteenth on the list of most nutritious vegetables, but they are first on the list of vegetables that Americans like most to eat.

(4)   But dislike is not the only reason why some cultures will not eat a certain food. In some cultures, certain foods are *taboo. Taboo* is a word from the language of the Fiji Islands that is used to describe something that is forbidden. (*Forbidden* means that you are not allowed to do it.) Some foods are taboo in certain religions, but there are also other food taboos that are not connected to a religion. We do not usually think about why certain things are taboo in our culture. We may not even know why they are taboo. Anthropologists try to discover the hidden reasons for taboos. For example, the sacred cows of India are well known. Cows can go wherever they want to in the streets of India, and they can eat anything they want from the supplies of the foodsellers on the street. As a result, the cows are a problem. However, no one in India will kill them or eat them. It is taboo to do so. This custom seems strange to other people, but anthropologists believe that there are reasons for it. First, cows are valuable because the farmers need them to help plow their fields. Second, cow manure is used as a fertilizer on the fields. In India, many farmers cannot

afford to spend money on fertilizer. Third, the cow manure can be dried and burned to make cooking fires. Therefore, farmers that kill their cows for meat soon find that they cannot plow or fertilize their fields or make a cooking fire.

(5)   Another example is that Americans do not eat dogs, although people from some other cultures regard them as good food. In the United States, dogs are very important to people as pets. They are usually regarded as part of the family, almost like a child in some cases. In addition, dogs have value as protection against criminals. Thieves will not usually enter a house where there is a dog because the dog will bark and possibly attack a stranger who is trying to get into a house. Apparently, the dog's place in society as a companion and as a protection against criminals makes the dog taboo as food.

(6)   The taboo against eating pork occurs in more than one culture. There is some evidence that some ancient Egyptians did not eat pork. The ancient Israelites also regarded pork as taboo. One explanation for the pig-eating taboo is that pork that is not cooked sufficiently may spread a disease called *trichinosis*. However, most people no longer think that this is a good explanation for the pork taboo. Another explanation is that the Israelites were nomads — they were always moving from place to place. People have to stay in one place to raise pigs. The Israelites did not want to stay in one place because they did not want to change their culture. As a result, they did not eat pigs.

(7)   Anthropologists believe that most food likes and dislikes are a result of the ways of life of different people. Some people live in areas where there are both large animals and many insects. It is difficult for these people to kill large animals, and it requires a lot of energy. It is easier for them to use insects for food because it is not difficult to catch insects and it does not require a lot of energy. Nomadic people who move around will not want to keep pigs for food. People will not eat pets such as dogs. Americans eat a lot of beef because there is plenty of land for raising cattle and their meat can be shipped cheaply for long distances by railroads.

EXERCISES

Scanning Questions

Look back in the reading selection for the answers to the following questions. Remember, write only the part of the sentence that is asked for. Do not write complete sentences.

Paragraph 1

1. What two ideas do we have about foods?

_____

_____

Paragraph 2

2. Who think that African termites make a delicious meal?

_____

3. What has more calories and protein than 100 grams of cooked hamburger?

_____

Paragraph 3

4. Which is first on a list of the most nutritious vegetables, broccoli or tomatoes?

_____

5. Which do Americans like to eat most, broccoli or tomatoes?

_____

Paragraph 4

6. What is the word *taboo* used to describe?

_____

7. What does *forbidden* mean?

_____

8. Where can cows go in the streets of India?

_____

9. What can the cows eat?

_____

10. Is it taboo to kill and eat cows in India?

_____

11. What will happen to farmers that kill their cows for meat?

_____

_____

Paragraph 5

12. Where are pet dogs usually regarded as part of the family?

_____

13. In addition to being pets, what value do dogs have?

_____

14. What makes dogs taboo as food in the United States?

_____

Paragraph 6

15. Who were the two ancient peoples who did not eat pork?

_____

16. Do nomads move from place to place, or do they stay in one place?

_____

Paragraph 7

17. What do anthropologists believe food likes and dislikes are the result of?

_____

Vocabulary

Below are a list of vocabulary words, followed by seven pairs of sentences.

Sentence **a** of each pair is from the reading selection. Look back in the reading selection and find the correct vocabulary word for sentence **a** of each pair.

Next, read sentence **b** carefully. On the blank line in sentence **b** of each pair, write the same word that you used in sentence **a**. Sentence **b** of each pair uses the same word as sentence **a** with the same meaning.

appropriate	forbidden	relate(d)	supply/supplies
common	problem	strange	

1a. Many people would find it disgusting to eat rats, but there are forty-two different cultures whose people regard rats as

_____ food.

b. It is not _____ to wear a bathing suit in a school class-room.

2a. However, food likes and dislikes do not always seem

_____ to nutrition.

b. On cold days, I wear warm clothes. On hot days I wear cool clothes.

The kind of clothes that I wear is _____ to the weather.

3a. For example, broccoli is first on a list of the most nutritious

_____ vegetables.

b. There are many cats with two colors. There are not many cats with

three colors. Two-colored cats are more _____ than three-colored cats.

4a. _Taboo_ is a word from the language of the Fiji Islands that is used to

describe something that is _____.

b. That sign on the wall says NO SMOKING. That means that we are

_____ to smoke in this room.

5a. Cows can go wherever they want to in the streets of India, and they

can eat anything that they want from the _____ of the foodsellers on the street.

b. Supermarkets have large _____ of many different kinds of food.

6a. As a result, the cows are a _____.

b. I had a _____ this morning. My car wouldn't start.

7a. This custom seems _____ to other people, but anthropologists believe that there are reasons for it.

b. January is a winter month in North America, but it is a summer month in Australia. If a North American goes to Australia in January, the warm weather there seems _____ to him.

Do the same with the following:

against	protection	require(s)	sufficiently
evidence	raising/raise	spread	

8a. In addition, dogs have value as _____ against criminals.

b. In cold weather, people wear warm clothes. The warm clothes provide _____ from the cold weather.

9a. In addition, the dogs have value as protection _____ criminals.

b. Now we know that too much sun can cause skin cancer, so many people wear special creams on their faces to protect them _____ getting too much sun.

10a. There is some _____ that some ancient Egyptians did not eat pork.

b. I walked into my kitchen. There was a loaf of bread, an open jar of peanut butter, and a dirty knife on the table. This _____ showed me that someone had made a peanut butter sandwich!

11a. One explanation for the pig-eating taboo is that pork that is not

cooked _____ may spread a disease called *trichinosis*.

b. It was very cold outside, and I was only wearing a sweater. I was

cold because I was not _____ dressed for the cold
weather.

12a. One explanation for the pig-eating taboo is that pork that is not

cooked sufficiently may _____ a disease called *trichi-nosis*.

b. In the past, people lived in small groups and did not see other
groups very often. So a sickness in one group could not

_____ to other groups. The other groups did not get
the sickness.

13a. It is difficult for these people to kill large animals, and it

_____ a lot of energy.

b. Learning a new language _____ hard work, studying,
and practice.

14a. Americans eat a lot of beef because there is plenty of land for

_____ cattle.

b. I buy young tomato plants for my garden. It is faster than

_____ tomatoes from seeds. It takes a long time to
grow tomatoes from seeds.

Self-Test

On the blank lines, write the correct words from the list below.

against	forbidden	related	strange
appropriate	problem	requires	sufficiently
common	protection	spread	supplies
evidence	raise		

1. Flies are very _____ in warm weather.

2. In some cultures, it is _____ to shake hands when you meet someone. In other cultures, however, people do not touch other people often, so they do not like to shake hands. It does not seem right to them.

3. In some cultures, a man is _____ to speak to his mother-in-law. He must not look at her either.

4. When people go mountain climbing, they must carry all their

    _____ with them.

5. The birds eat the seeds in my garden, so nothing grows. The birds

    are a _____.

6. Small cars use less gas than large cars. The amount of gas that a car

    uses is _____ to its size.

7. The sun does not shine in the Arctic for six months a year. It is al-

    ways dark then. I think that is _____.

8. When it rains, we carry an umbrella for _____ from the rain.

9. Anthropologists have found plant seeds from prehistoric times. From

   this _____, they can tell us what prehistoric people
   ate.

10. You can't drive a car without a driver's license. The law

    _____ you to have a driver's license.

11. We buy automobile insurance _____ the possibility of
    an accident, which might cost a lot of money.

12. Some people move to the suburbs because they do not want to

    _____ children in the city.

13. I put too much water in my plant. The water dripped down the side of

    the pot and _____ over the table.

14. My plant died because I didn't water it _____.

Adjective Clauses

A clause is a group of words that contains a subject and a verb that shows
time.

Examples:

a and **b** are *independent* clauses. They are complete sentences.

   a. I walked down the street.
      The subject is *I* and the verb **walked** shows past time.
   b. It is raining.
      The subject is *It* and the verb **is raining** shows present time.

Examples:

c and **d** are *dependent* clauses. They are not complete sentences. They need something added to them to make complete sentences.

    c. because it is raining
    d. that an animal is born with

In **c** the signal word *because* makes this a dependent clause. We need to add an independent clause to make **c** a complete sentence.

<u>**We can't have a picnic**</u> **because it is raining.**

d is a dependent adjective clause. Adjective clauses modify nouns and noun phrases. That means that they describe, limit, or add to the meaning of nouns and noun phrases.

Adjective clauses follow the noun or noun phrase:

Instinctive behavior is a pattern of behavior <u>**that an**</u>

<u>**animal is born with.**</u>

In the above sentence, the adjective clause **that an animal is born with** modifies the noun phrase **a pattern of behavior**.

    Question: What is instinctive behavior?
    Answer: A pattern of behavior that an animal is born with.

Adjective clauses frequently begin with one of the following words:

    people   **who, whom, that**
    things   **that, which**
    places   **where, in which**
    time   **when**

Look at the following sentences:

    a. **We may laugh at clothing that seems ridiculous to us.**
        The adjective clause is <u>that seems ridiculous to us.</u>

        It modifies the noun <u>clothing.</u>

        What kind of clothing may we laugh at?
        Clothing that seems ridiculous to us

    b. However, the way in which they take care of these needs depends on the culture in which they grow up.

There are two adjective clauses in the above sentence.

    The first one — **in which they take care of these needs** — modifies the word way.

    What depends on the culture in which they grow up? The way in which they take care of these needs.

    The second clause — **in which they grow up** — modifies the word culture.

    What does the way in which they take care of these needs depend on? The culture in which they grow up.

Read each of the sentences below. Draw a line under each adjective clause. Draw a circle around the word or words that each clause modifies. Then answer the questions.

1. As a result, people from one culture often think the foods that people from another culture eat are disgusting or nauseating.

   What do people from one culture often think are disgusting or nauseating? _____

2. For example, broccoli is first on a list of the most nutritious common vegetables, but it is twenty-first on a list of vegetables that Americans like most to eat.

   What list is broccoli twenty-first on?

   _____

3. *Taboo* is a word from the language of the Fiji Islands that is used to describe something that is forbidden.

   What do Fiji Islanders use the word *taboo* to describe?

   _____

4. Therefore, farmers that kill their cows for meat soon find they cannot plow or fertilize their fields or make a cooking fire.

   What farmers soon find they cannot plow or fertilize their fields or make a cooking fire? _____

5. One explanation for the pig-eating taboo is that pork that is not cooked sufficiently may spread a disease called *trichinosis*.

What kind of pork may spread a disease called *trichinosis*?

_____

Signal Words

Some words do not really have meaning in themselves. They are used as *signals* to show the relationship of one part of a sentence to another part of the sentence, or to show the relationship between sentences in a paragraph, or even to show the relationship between paragraphs.

⟫ *Example*

For example   The words **for example** are a signal. They tell the reader that the sentence with the words **for example** is an example of a more general statement.

Look at the following sentences from the reading selection:

> **As a result, people from one culture often think the foods that people from another culture eat are disgusting or nauseating. When the famous boxer Muhammad Ali visited Africa,** *for example*, **one member of his group became quite sick when he saw someone pick up a butterfly and eat it.**

The first sentence is a general statement — some foods that other people eat can make us sick. The second sentence gives a specific example — a specific person became sick when he saw someone eat a butterfly.

Read the sentences below carefully and answer the questions.

1. Food likes and dislikes do not seem related to nutrition. For example, broccoli is first on a list of the most nutritious common vegetables, but it is twenty-first on a list of vegetables that Americans like most to eat.

What is the general statement?

_____

Is broccoli the most nutritious common vegetable? _____

Is it the most popular vegetable with Americans? _____

Is broccoli an example of a food like (or dislike) that is not related to

nutrition? _____

2. In paragraph 4, the following sentence is a general statement:

    Anthropologists try to discover the reasons for taboos.

    The rest of the paragraph is an example. It describes a taboo. What is
    the taboo? (Circle the letter of the correct answer.)

    a. Cows go wherever they want to in India.
    b. Cows are a problem in India.
    c. No one will kill cows in India.

    Then the paragraph gives anthropologists' reasons for this taboo.
    First it gives reasons why cows are valuable in India.

    How many reasons are there? _____

    What words signal the reasons? _____

    The last sentence of this paragraph is the anthropologists' conclu-
    sion as to why people do not kill the cows.

Contrast/Unexpected Information

but,   These words signal a contrast between two clauses
although,   in one sentence or between two sentences.
however,
on the other hand

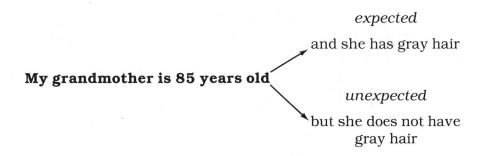

Most people have gray hair when they are 85 years old. We expect them to have gray hair. We are surprised if they do not have gray hair. The word **but** signals that we are going to read some information that we do not expect. **But** usually joins two independent clauses.

We can write the above sentence with **although**.

> **My grandmother does not have gray hair although she is 85 years old.**

In this sentence, the clause with **although** is a dependent clause. **However** cannot be used to join two clauses. You must have two separate sentences:

> **My grandmother is 85 years old. However, she does not have gray hair.**

or you can join the two clauses with a semicolon:

> **My grandmother is 85 years old; however, she does not have gray hair.**

Read the following sentences and answer the questions.

1. Many people would find it disgusting to eat rats, but there are forty-two different cultures whose people regard rats as appropriate food.

    What is the unexpected information? (Circle the letter of the correct answer.)
       a. Many people would find it disgusting to eat rats.
       b. Some people regard rats as appropriate food.

2. For example, broccoli is first on a list of the most nutritious common vegetables, but it is twenty-first on a list of vegetables that Americans like most to eat.

    What is the unexpected information?
       a. The most nutritious vegetable is not the most popular vegetable in America.
       b. The most popular vegetable in America is also the most nutritious vegetable.

3. Many other people would probably be sick if they had to eat termites, but one hundred grams of termites contain more than twice
   as many calories and almost twice as much protein as one hundred
   grams of cooked hamburger.

   What is the unexpected information?

   a. Many people do not want to eat termites.
   b. Termites are a nutritious food.

4. Another example is that Americans do not eat dogs, although
   people from some other cultures regard them as good food.

   What is the contrast?

   a. Some people eat dogs. Some people do not eat dogs.
   b. Americans do not eat dogs. Other people do not eat dogs.

Comprehension Questions

Answer the following questions by drawing a circle around **True** or **False**, by drawing a circle
around the letter of the correct answer, or by writing the answer on the blank line. If a
statement is false, explain why it is false.

Paragraph 1

1. Why did one member of Muhammad Ali's group become sick when
   he saw someone eat a butterfly?

   a. He didn't like that particular kind of butterfly.
   b. He ate some bad food.
   c. Butterflies are not appropriate food in his culture.

2. **True** or **False** Some cultures do not regard rats as appropriate food.

Paragraph 3

3. In line 3, the word "it" refers to

   a. broccoli
   b. list
   c. vegetables

4. In line 5, "they" refers to

   a. Americans
   b. list
   c. tomatoes

5. What list are tomatoes first on?

   _____

6. **True** or **False** People always prefer the most nutritious food.

Paragraph 4

7. **True** or **False** We always know why certain things are taboo in our culture.

8. In line 12, the word "However" signals unexpected information. What is the unexpected information?

   a. Cows are a problem.
   b. No one in India will kill or eat cows (although they are a problem).
   c. This custom seems strange to other people.

9. In line 19, "they" refers to

   a. farmers
   b. cows
   c. farmers that kill their cows for meat

Paragraph 5

10. In line 2, "them" refers to

    a. Americans
    b. dogs
    c. people from other cultures

11. In line 3, "They" refers to _____

12. Who will a dog possibly attack?_____

13. **True** or **False** Some people in some cultures regard dogs as appropriate food.

Paragraph 6

14. What kind of pork may spread trichinosis?

_____

Paragraph 7

15. In line 4, "it" refers to

    a. difficult
    b. people
    c. to kill large animals

16. Americans eat a lot of beef because

    a. there is lots of land for raising cattle in the United States
    b. the meat from cattle can be shipped cheaply for long distances
    c. both **a** and **b**

✍ Writing Assignment: Summary of a Paragraph

A summary of a paragraph is shorter than the original paragraph. A summary should contain the main information in the paragraph and one or two details about the main information. When you write a summary, you must write sentences of your own. You do not copy sentences from the paragraph.

One way to learn to write a summary is as follows:

Step 1   Read the paragraph from Chapter 1 below carefully.

The word culture has many different meanings. For example, we sometimes say that people who know about art, music, and literature are cultured. However, the word culture has a different meaning for anthropologists (people who study humankind). To an anthropologist, the word culture means all the ways in which a group of people act, dress, think, and feel. People have to learn the cultural ways of their community; they are not something that the people in the group are born with.

Step 2 Read the paragraph a second time. This time, draw a line under any words or short groups of words that you think are important.

IIII➡ *Example*

The word <u>culture</u> has many <u>different meanings</u>. For example, we <u>sometimes say that people who know</u> about art, music, and literature are cultured. However, the word culture has a different meaning for <u>anthropologists</u> (people who study humankind). To an anthropologist, the word culture means <u>all the ways</u> in which a <u>group</u> of people <u>act</u>, <u>dress</u>, <u>think</u>, and <u>feel</u>. <u>People</u> have to <u>learn</u> the <u>cultural ways</u> of their <u>community</u>; they are <u>not</u> something that the people in the group are <u>born with</u>.

Step 3 On a separate piece of paper, write the words and groups of words that you underlined.

IIII➡ *Example*

culture	feel
different meanings	people
anthropologists	learn
all the ways	cultural ways
group	community
act	not
dress	born with
think	

Step 4 Discuss the above list of words with a partner. Do you agree with this list? Would you use different words? What are they?

Step 5 Now close your book. Write a summary of the paragraph using the list of words and groups of words to help you.

⟫ *Example*

Culture has different meanings. For anthropologists, culture is all the ways people do things, like thinking and feeling. People learn the cultural ways in their community. People are not born with these ways.

Discuss the following with a partner:

- Is this summary shorter than the original paragraph from Chapter 1?
- Does this summary contain the important information from the original paragraph?
- Would you add other information? If so, why?

Now write a summary of paragraph 5 of the reading selection in this chapter.

Step 1   Read paragraph 5 of the reading selection carefully.

Step 2   Read paragraph 5 a second time. This time, draw a line under any words or short groups of words that you think are important.

Step 3   On a separate piece of paper, write the words and groups of words that you underlined.

Step 4   Compare your list of words with a partner or in a small group. Discuss any differences. Do you want to make any changes in your list? Is your list too short or too long or just right?

Step 5   Now close your book. Use your list of words to help you write a summary of paragraph 5.

Reports of cannibalism among some tribes may be exaggerated,
but this custom is known to exist. *Courtesy of the American
Museum of Natural History.*

3	# Cannibalism

In small groups, discuss the following questions:

- What is cannibalism?
- Have you ever read or heard any stories about cannibalism? What were they?
- What kind of people are cannibals?
- Is there more than one kind of cannibalism? Is it always bad?
- Why do people eat other people or parts of other people?

READING SELECTION

Cannibalism

Some five hundred years or so ago, Europeans began to explore the rest of the world with their sailing ships. They discovered many lands and people, and the people that they discovered had many new customs. Because the Europeans knew only their own culture, most of them thought that these newly discovered peoples and their cultures and customs were disgusting or wrong. One of the customs that most shocked the Europeans was that of cannibalism or people eating other people.

(2)   There seem to be three kinds of cannibalism. There is the kind that happens when a group of people is isolated from other people and has no other source of food. One example was survivors of a plane crash high in the mountains who were not found for several weeks. It can also happen with people in a life raft at sea after a shipwreck. In these situations, as people die of starvation, their bodies are eaten by those who are still alive.

(3)   A second kind of cannibalism occurs when the bodies or parts of the bodies of friends or relatives are eaten. Often only a particular part — the heart or bones — is eaten. This part is often burned and then ground up, and the ashes are then used in a drink. This is usually cannibalism of a special kind. This kind of cannibalism obviously has no nutritional value. The idea behind it seems to be to have some sort of continuity with the dead. Some peoples believe that it is possible to acquire the bravery or intelligence of dead people by a ceremonial eating of a small part of their bodies.

(4)   The third kind of cannibalism is the killing and eating of enemies for food. This is what most people think of when they think of cannibalism. Nevertheless, at least one anthropologist believes that there has never been cannibalism of this kind. According to this anthropologist, the reports of cannibalism arise because one tribe of people describes another tribe as evil. It is always someone else who is a cannibal, not the tribe that is speaking. There have been a number of supposedly eye-witness reports of cannibalism. However, people who do not believe that there has ever been any kind of cannibalism say that some reason can be found to doubt these reports.

(5)   It is probably quite true that many reports of cannibalism were exaggerated or false. Undoubtedly, in the early days of European exploration, many explorers simply called all dark-skinned peoples "cannibals."

Thinking of these people as cannibals gave the Europeans an excuse for the bad way that they treated many of these people by killing or enslaving them.

(6)   In spite of this, many people believe that cannibalism existed under certain situations. A number of seemingly reliable witnesses in the sixteenth and seventeenth centuries (1500–1700) have reported it. It was probably not common, however, because those people who practice cannibalism do not often capture prisoners in a war, and it was these prisoners who were the usual victims.

(7)   People in present-day societies do not usually practice cannibalism. This is not because people today are any nicer than people used to be. What seems to have happened as history progressed is that prisoners of war became more valuable as slaves than they were as meat. Now, even the enslavement of prisoners of war is rare, although it has happened, as, for example, in Germany in World War II.

(8)   There was one large and complex society that was unusual because they used humans as food. It was that of the Aztecs of Mexico, who lived four hundred to seven hundred years ago. Victims were taken to the tops of the Aztec pyramids where they were held by four priests while a fifth cut out the victims' hearts. The body was then pushed down the stairs to the base of the pyramid where it was cut up for eating. In this way, the Aztecs killed between 15,000 and 25,000 people a year.

(9)   Were the Aztecs particularly savage? Perhaps not. A number of anthropologists believe that there was a continual shortage of animals for food in the valley of Mexico. As a result, the Aztecs ate human flesh because it was a source of meat and protein for them.

EXERCISES

Scanning Questions

Look back in the reading selection for the answers to the following questions. Remember, write only what is asked for.

Paragraph 1

1. Who discovered many lands and people?

   _____

2. Who had many new customs?

   _____

3. What is cannibalism?

   _____

Paragraph 2

4. When does one kind of cannibalism happen?

   _____

5. What are two examples of this kind of cannibalism?

   _____

Paragraph 3

6. When does a second kind of cannibalism occur?

   _____

7. What does the idea behind this kind of cannibalism seem to be?

    _____

8. What do some people believe it is possible to acquire by a ceremonial eating of a small part of the bodies of friends or relatives?

    _____

Paragraph 4

9. What is the third kind of cannibalism?

    _____

10. What do most people think of when they think of cannibalism? (What does "This" refer to?)

    _____

11. According to one anthropologist, what causes reports of cannibalism?

    _____

12. Who say that some reason can be found to doubt the eye-witness reports of cannibalism?

    _____

Paragraph 5

13. What is probably quite true?

    _____

14. What gave the Europeans an excuse for the bad way in which they treated many dark-skinned people?

    _____

Paragraph 6

15. In Line 3, what do "it" and "It" refer to? (They both refer to the same thing.)

_____

Paragraph 7

16. Who do not usually practice cannibalism?

_____

17. What seems to have happened to prisoners of war as history progressed?

_____

Paragraph 8

18. What large and complex society was unusual because it used humans as food?

_____

Paragraph 9

19. What was human flesh a source of for the Aztecs?

_____

Vocabulary

Below are a list of seven vocabulary words and seven pairs of sentences. Fill in the blanks with the correct words. Remember: Sentence **a** of each pair is from the reading selection. Sentence **b** of each pair uses the same word as sentence **a** with the same meaning.

continuity	isolate(d)	situation(s)	supposedly
doubt	obviously	source	isolate(d)

1a. There is the kind (of cannibalism) that happens when a group of

people is _____ from other people and has no other
source of food.

  b. There aren't any other houses near our house. Our house is

_____.

2a. There is the kind that happens when a group of people is isolated

from other people and has no other _____ of food.

  b. Some people get their water from wells (holes in the ground). The

wells are the people's _____ of water.

3a. In these _____, as people die of starvation, their
bodies are eaten by those who are still alive.

  b. I am in a difficult _____. I have lost my airplane
ticket, and my plane will leave in a few minutes.

4a. This kind of cannibalism _____ has no nutritional
value.

  b. He wears expensive clothes, he has three gold watches, and his car

is a Ferrari. He _____ has a lot of money.

5a. The idea behind it seems to be to have some sort of

_____ with the dead.

  b. When the President of the United States dies, the Vice-President
becomes President immediately. This provides for the

_____ of the American government.

6a. There have been a number of _____ eye-witness
reports of cannibalism.

    b. According to some scientists, the temperatures on earth are

_____ going to get hotter. However, other scientists say that this may not be true.

7a. However, people who do not believe that there has ever been any kind of cannibalism say that some reason can be found to

_____ these reports.

    b. Some scientists say that the earth is supposedly going to get hotter.

However, other scientists _____ that this will happen.

Do the same with the following:

capture(d)	exaggerate(d)	savage	treat(ed)
certain	reliable	shortage	

8a. It is probably quite true that many reports of cannibalism were

_____ or false.

    b. He told us that many people died in the fire. That was an

_____ amount. Only three people died.

9a. Thinking of these people as cannibals gave the Europeans an excuse for the bad way that they _____ many of these people by killing or enslaving them.

    b. When John asked Mary to marry him, she _____ him very unkindly. She laughed and told him to go away.

10a. In spite of this, many people believe that cannibalism existed under

_____ situations.

   b. She only eats _____ kinds of meat. She eats chicken and lamb, but she doesn't eat pork or beef.

11a. A number of seemingly _____ witnesses in the sixteenth and seventeenth centuries (1500–1700) have reported it.

   b. Our mailman comes every day at 10:00 a.m. You can depend on him. He is very _____.

12a. It was probably not common, however, because those people who practice cannibalism do not often _____ prisoners in a war, and it was these prisoners who were the usual victims.

   b. A monkey got out of its cage at the zoo yesterday. The zoo keepers _____ it and put it back in its cage.

13a. Were the Aztecs particularly _____?

   b. The killer stabbed the victim thirty times. It was a very _____ killing.

14a. A number of anthropologists believe that there was a continual _____ of animals for food in the valley of Mexico.

   b. There are twenty-five students in the classroom, but there are only eighteen chairs. There is a _____ of chairs for this class.

Self-Test

Fill in the blank lines with the correct words from the list below.

captured	doubt	obviously	shortage	supposedly
certain	exaggerated	reliable	situation	treated
continuity	isolated	savage	source	

1. My son said that he was late for school because there were ten elephants walking down the street. I _____ it! There aren't any elephants in our town!

2. When people get certain sicknesses, they are _____ from other people. This way, other people will not get the sickness.

3. Some people begin to study a new language. They study it for a few weeks. Then they stop studying it. Then they start to study it again. Then they stop again for a few weeks. This is not a good way to learn a new language. You must not start and stop this way. It is important to have _____ when you are learning a new language.

4. According to the newspaper, there was a big fire last night. The words "According to the newspaper" tell us that the newspaper is the _____ of the information about the fire.

5. When I woke up this morning, the sun was shining, but the streets and sidewalks were wet. It _____ rained during the night.

6. According to the weather man, it is _____ going to rain today. I doubt it. The sun is shining, and there aren't any clouds.

7. Sometimes I don't know all the answers on a test. In this _____, I usually try to guess some answers.

8. John always does a good job. He is very _____.

9. Some zoo animals are born in the zoo. Others are

    _____ in the wild and then brought to the zoo.

10. When the American writer Mark Twain was still alive, he read in a
    newspaper that he was dead. He wrote to the newspaper and said,

    "The reports of my death have been greatly _____."

11. Do you only like _____ kinds of books, such as mys-
    teries, or do you like a lot of different kinds of stories?

12. We used to think that gorillas were _____ animals.
    Now we know that they are very gentle.

13. I stayed with a family in another country for two weeks. They

    _____ me very well. I had a wonderful time.

14. So many people were hurt in the earthquake that there was a

    _____ of medical supplies to take care of them.

Signal Words: Cause and Result

Cause

because
   The word **because** signals a cause or reason. The clause
with **because** is a dependent clause. It tells us the cause or
reason for the action or information in the independent
clause. It answers the question "**Why**."

Look at the following sentence:

**The Chinese used to bind women's feet because they
regarded small feet as beautiful.**

Why did the Chinese bind women's feet?

because they regarded small feet as beautiful

When we use **because**, the dependent clause can also come before the independent clause.

Because the women could not walk very well, they couldn't do much housework.

Why couldn't the women do much housework?

because they could not walk very well

Now look at these sentences from the reading selection in this chapter. Draw a line under each dependent **cause** clause. Then answer the questions.

1. Because the Europeans knew only their own culture, most of them thought that these newly discovered peoples and their cultures and customs were disgusting or wrong.

   Why did the Europeans think that these newly discovered peoples and their cultures and customs were disgusting or wrong?

   _____

2. It (cannibalism) was probably not common, however, because those people who practice cannibalism do not often capture prisoners in a war, and it was these prisoners who were the usual victims.

   Why was cannibalism probably not common?

   _____

3. There was one large and complex society that was unusual because they used humans for food. It was that of the Aztecs of Mexico, who lived four hundred to seven hundred years ago.

   Why were the Aztecs of Mexico an unusual complex society?

   _____

Result/Effect

so   The word **so** is used to join two independent clauses. The
              clause that follows **so** tells the result/effect of the action or
              information in the first clause.

Look at the following sentence:

**The Flathead Indians of North America wanted their chil-
dren to have long sloping foreheads, so they used to bind
the heads of babies.**

What was the result of the Flathead Indians wanting their children to
have long sloping foreheads?

They used to bind the heads of their babies.

When we use **so**, the first clause is the cause/reason. Why did the Flathead Indians bind the heads of their babies?

They wanted them to have long sloping foreheads.

Read the following sentences. Draw a line under the result clause. Then answer the
questions.

1. Europeans knew only their own culture, so most of them thought
   that these newly discovered peoples and their cultures and customs
   were wrong.

   What was the result of the fact that Europeans knew only their own
   culture?

   _____

   _____

   Why did most Europeans think that these newly discovered peoples
   and their cultures and customs were wrong?

   _____

2. Those people who practice cannibalism do not often capture prisoners in a war, and it was these prisoners who were the usual victims, so cannibalism was probably not common.

   What was the result of the fact that people who practice cannibalism
   do not often capture prisoners in a war?

   _____

   Why was cannibalism probably not common?

   _____

The following words also signal a result/effect:

   therefore   as a result   thus

They do not join two clauses.

Read the following sentences and answer the questions:

1. The kinds of food that we eat and the way that we prepare them and
   eat them are all part of our culture. *As a result*, people from one culture often think that the foods that people from another culture eat
   are disgusting or nauseating.

   Why do people from one culture often think that the foods that people from another culture eat are disgusting or nauseating?

   _____

   _____

   What is the result of the fact that the kinds of food that we eat and the
   way that we prepare them and eat them are all part of our culture?

   _____

   _____

2. Cattle can go wherever they want to in the streets of India, and they can eat anything that they want from the supplies of the foodsellers on the street. *As a result*, the cows are a problem.

What is the result of the fact that cows can go wherever they want to in the streets of India, and they can eat anything that they want from the supplies of the foodsellers on the street?

_____

Why are cows a problem in India?

_____

_____

3. It is not difficult to catch insects, and it does not require a lot of energy. *Therefore*, it is easier for these people to use insects for food.

What is the result sentence?

_____

Why is it easier for these people to use insects for food?

_____

Word Families

Listed on the next page are different forms of some of the vocabulary words in Chapters 1, 2, and 3. These new forms are different parts of speech. Study them before doing the exercises.

Verbs	Nouns	Adjectives	Adverbs
——	——	appropriate	appropriately
attract	attractiveness	attractive	——
depend	——	dependent	——
exaggerate	exaggeration	——	——
isolate	isolation	isolated	——
protect	protection	protective	——
rely	reliance	reliable	——

We form the antonyms (opposites) of some adjectives by adding a prefix. *Prefixes are added to the beginning of a word.*

un-, in- (+ adjective)

> unattractive = not attractive   inappropriate = not appropriate
> unreliable   = not reliable   independent   = not dependent

Noun endings	**-ness, -ence, -ance, -tion**
Verb ending	**-ate**
Adjective endings	**-able/-ible, -ive**

Write the correct form of each word on the blank lines.

1.   appropriate   inappropriate   appropriately

   a. It is _____ to wear a bathing suit in a classroom.

   b. You should dress _____ for the classroom.

   c. In some cultures, it is _____ to write a letter of sympathy to the family of someone who has died. The family is pleased to get the letter.

2.   attract   attractiveness   attractive   unattractive

   a. What do you think is more important in a person you marry —

      intelligence or _____?

   b. Some male birds do dances to _____ female birds.

c. Some new fashions are very _____ and look nice on people.

d. However, many new fashions don't look nice on anyone. They are

very _____.

3.   depend   dependent   independent

a. Usually students' grades for a course _____ on their test scores.

b. Sometimes students don't have tests in a course. They are required to write a research paper instead. Then their grades are

_____ on the quality of the research paper.

c. Sometimes a student can do an _____ study. In this case, the student does not attend a class. This kind of study is not related to classwork.

4.   exaggerate   exaggeration   exaggerated

a. The fisherman said that he caught a five-foot-long fish. This was

an _____. The fish was only one foot long!

b. The length of the fish was _____.

c. Fishermen sometimes like to _____.

5.   isolate   isolation   isolated

a. Some people _____ themselves from other people. They do not like to live near other people.

b. However, _____ is not good for everyone. Some people get very unhappy if they cannot see other people often.

c. Would you like to live in an _____ area, or do you prefer to be near friends and neighbors?

6.   protect   protection   protective

   a. Some mothers are very _____ of their children. They do not want their children to get hurt, so they watch their children carefully.

   b. We should eat a good diet to _____ our health.

   c. A paper umbrella would not be a good _____ from the rain.

7.   rely   reliance   reliable

   a. _____ on a bilingual dictionary is not always a good idea, although it is helpful sometimes.

   b. John always tells the truth. You can _____ on what he says.

   c. In other words, John is a very _____ person.

Comprehension Questions

Answer the following questions by circling the word **True** or the word **False**. If a statement is false, explain why. For one question, you must write your answer on the blank lines.

1. True or **False**   Cannibalism was not a European custom.

2. In the first kind of cannibalism, what are two situations in which, as people die of starvation, their bodies are eaten by those who are still alive?

   _____

   _____

3. True or **False**   In the second kind of cannibalism, parts of the body are eaten for their nutritional value.

4. **True** or **False**   At least one anthropologist does not believe that people have killed and eaten their enemies for food.

5. **True** or **False**   Some people doubt the eye-witness reports of the third kind of cannibalism.

6. **True** or **False**   Europeans enslaved and killed many dark-skinned people that they met in the early days of European exploration.

7. **True** or **False**   The victims of the third kind of cannibalism were usually the friends and relatives of the primitive peoples.

8. **True** or **False**   People in present-day societies do not eat their enemies because they are nicer than people used to be.

9. **True** or **False**   The Aztecs possibly ate human flesh for its nutritional value.

✍ Writing Assignment

Reread each paragraph and write one question for each paragraph. After you write your questions, find a partner. Ask each other the questions that you wrote. Look at the reading to find the answers to your partner's questions and answer them orally. Do not write the answers.

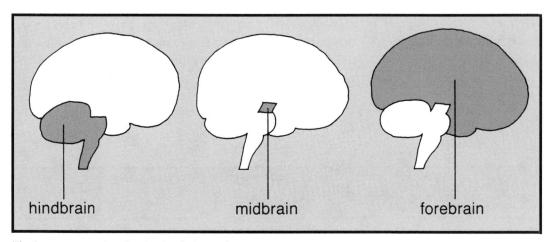

hindbrain   midbrain   forebrain

The brain is considered to be divided into three major parts,
namely, the hindbrain, the midbrain, and the forebrain. *Reprinted
with the permission of Houghton-Mifflin Co., from* The Amazing
Brain, *by Robert Ornstein and Richard F. Thompson. Illustration
by David Macaulay.*

4 The Three-Pound Miracle

- What do you know about the human brain?
- How big is it?
- What does it look like?
- Is it all one piece, or does it have parts?

Work with a partner or in small groups. On the map below, write information about the brain under each separate heading:

> Size
> Appearance (what does it look like?)
> Parts
> Functions (What does the brain do?)
> Other (What else do you know about the brain?)

Do not write complete sentences. If you don't have the information, make some guesses. When everyone is finished, combine the information from each group on the board.

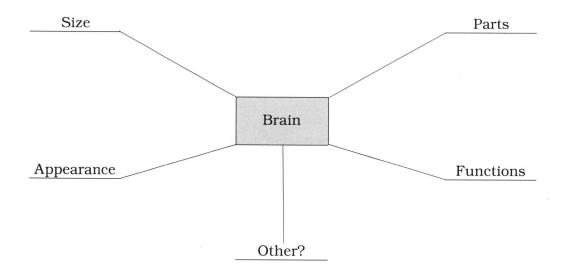

What does <u>vertebrate</u> mean? Name some vertebrate animals. The opposite of vertebrate is invertebrate. Squids, spiders, and shrimp are examples of invertebrate animals. Name some other invertebrates.

When we want to move, or pick something up, or sit down, and so on, we send a message to the brain. How do our bodies send messages to the brain? How does the brain send commands to our muscles so that we can move or pick something up, or sit down?

There are some things that our bodies do for us that we don't have to think about. The brain causes us to do these things without a command from us. Can you think of any things that our bodies do without our thinking about them?

In this reading selection, you will see the following Greek and Latin words:

cerebrum
cerebellum
corpus callosum
hypothalamus
medulla oblongata
pineal
thalamus

These words are simply names for different parts of the brain just like **head**, **hand**, and **leg** are English names for different parts of the body.

READING SELECTION

The Three-Pound Miracle

The brain of a human being is only a small part of the human body, but it is an extremely important one. The human brain weighs only about three pounds and looks like a mass of jelly. The volume of the brain is about three pints (in metric units about 1500 cubic centimeters [cc]). This is because a pound of water has a volume of one pint, and the brain, like the rest of the human body, contains a good deal of water. Yet there is a computer in that three-pound jelly-like mass. The computer in the human brain is more powerful and more complicated than any computer that scientists and engineers have been able to build.

(2)   Not all animal brains are as large or as complicated as the human brain. All vertebrates (vertebrates are animals with skeletons and backbones) have brains, but their brains are not all the same size. The brains of primitive vertebrates such as fish, frogs, and snakes are much smaller than the human brain, and they are tube-like in shape. These tube-like brains have three parts of about equal size: the forebrain, the midbrain, and the hindbrain.

(3)   Mammals are higher vertebrates which are warm blooded and nurse their young. Some examples of mammals are elephants, deer, dogs, mice, and people. They have brains that are somewhat different from the brains of primitive vertebrates. The forebrain is greatly developed in mammals, especially a part called the *cerebrum*. Human beings are mammals, and they have an extremely large cerebrum. This cerebrum is divided into two cerebral hemispheres. (A sphere is a round ball, and a hemisphere is half of a sphere.) There is a bridge of tissue called the *corpus callosum* between the two hemispheres.

(4)   The cerebrum is located in the forebrain. It is the largest and one of the most important parts of the brain. However, there are other parts to the forebrain, particularly a group of organs called the *limbic system*. The human midbrain is small and folded inside the rest of the brain, so it is difficult to see. The hindbrain has two important parts, the *medulla oblongata* and the *cerebellum*. These are at the bottom rear of the brain, near the place where it is attached to the spinal cord. There are also a number of small glands located in the brain. The *thalamus* and *hypothalamus* are two of these. Another one is a tiny gland called the *pineal* gland. The French philosopher René Descartes thought that it was the place

where the body was in contact with the soul. We now think the pineal gland was once a third eye that our reptilian ancestors had millions of years ago. The tuatara, a strange lizard-like animal that lives only in New Zealand, has a pineal gland that functions as a third eye. This third eye is able to distinguish light and darkness.

(5)   The human brain is a computer (when *it* is computing *we* are thinking). It is also a switchboard and command center as well. It receives messages from our eyes, ears, nose and tongue. It also receives impulses telling us when we are touching things. When our body is injured, it sends a message of pain to the brain. All these messages go to the brain through the nervous system. The nervous system consists of special cells called *nerve cells*. Messages and commands are sent from one cell to another by electrical impulses.

(6)   The brain itself consists of about 50 billion nerve cells. Each one of these cells is in touch with 10,000 other brain cells. From the brain, messages travel out through a part of the nervous system called the *spinal cord*. The spinal cord consists of many nerve cells which form a long string or fiber inside our backbones (*spines*). From the spinal cord, nerves travel out to various parts of the body, all the way to the tips of our fingers and toes. The brain sends commands through the nervous system to our muscles and causes us to walk, run, pick something up, shake hands, and so on. Actions like running or picking something up require thinking. We do these things on purpose.

(7)   The brain and the nervous system also cause us to do some things without thinking — such as breathing or digesting our food. We do not have to command our brains to do these things. We also do not have to command our hearts to beat because the brain and the nervous system do it for us. Breathing and digesting our food are called *autonomous functions*, and they occur whether or not we think about them.

(8)   Scientists know less about the brain than they do about most other parts of the body. However, they have learned some things about the brain, and in the next two readings you will read about what they have learned.

EXERCISES

Scanning Questions

Look back at the reading selection and find the answers to the following questions.

Paragraph 1

1. What looks like a mass of jelly?

   _____

2. What is the volume of the brain?

   _____

3. What is the volume of a pound of water?

   _____

Paragraph 2

4. What are vertebrates?

   _____

5. What are some primitive vertebrates?

   _____

6. What are the three parts of the tube-like brains (of primitive vertebrates)?

   _____

Paragraph 3

7. What are some examples of mammals?

_____

8. What is a sphere?

_____

9. What is a hemisphere?

_____

Paragraph 4

10. What are the three main divisions of the human brain?

_____

11. In the tuatara, what does the pineal gland function as?

_____

Paragraph 5

12. How do messages go to our brains?

_____

13. What does the nervous system consist of?

_____

14. How are messages and commands sent from one cell to another?

_____

Paragraph 6

15. How many nerve cells does the brain consist of?

_____

16. What does the spinal cord consist of?

_____

17. What are some actions that require thinking?

_____

Paragraph 7

18. What are some things that we do without thinking?

_____

19. What kind of functions are breathing and digesting our food called?

_____

Vocabulary

Below are seven pairs of sentences. Sentence **a** of each pair is from the reading selection. Look back at the reading and find the correct word for sentence **a**. Write it on the blank line in **a**. Then read sentence **b** carefully. Write the word from sentence **a** on the blank line in sentence **b**. This word has the same meaning in both sentences.

complicated	develop(ed)	located	volume
contain(s)	function(s)	primitive	

1a. The _____ of the brain is about three pints (in metric units about 1500 cubic centimeters [cc]).

b. Ten books fit in the blue box. Only five books fit in the green box.

The blue box has a larger _____ than the green box.

2a. This is because a pound of water has a volume of one pint, and the

brain, like the rest of the human body, _____ a good deal of water.

b. The blue box can _____ more books than the green box.

3a. The computer in the human brain is more powerful and more

_____ than any computer that scientists and engineers have been able to build.

b. A word-processor is more _____ than a typewriter.

4a. The brains of _____ vertebrates such as fish, frogs, and snakes are much smaller than the human brain, and they are tube-like in shape.

b. We usually dig holes with a shovel. Sometimes children dig holes

with a stick. Then the stick is a _____ type of shovel.

5a. The forebrain is greatly _____ in mammals, especially a part called the *cerebrum*.

b. A new-born baby cannot sit up or stand up because its muscles are

not _____ enough yet.

6a. There are also a number of small glands _____ in the brain.

b. The business district is usually _____ in the center of a city.

7a. The tuatara, a strange, lizard-like animal that lives only in New

Zealand, has a pineal gland that _____ as a third eye.

b. The _____ of an elevator is to carry people up and down in tall buildings.

Do the same with the following:

consist(s) (of)   form   message(s)   various
distinguish   impulse(s)   occur(s)

8a. This third eye is able to _____ light and darkness.

b. Jean and Mary are twins. They look exactly the same. I can't

_____ which is Jean and which is Mary!

9a. It receives _____ from our eyes, ears, nose, and tongue.

b. When I am not home, callers can leave a _____ on my phone answering machine.

10a. Messages and commands are sent from one cell to another by elec-

trical _____.

b. When you push a doorbell with your finger, an electrical

_____ causes the bell to ring.

11a. The brain itself _____ of about 50 billion nerve cells.

b. A good foreign language program _____ of grammar, reading, writing, and conversation.

12a. The spinal cord consists of many nerve cells which

_____ a long string or fiber inside our backbones (*spines*).

b. Children like to play with soft clay. They can _____ the clay into different shapes.

13a. From the spinal cord, nerves travel out to _____ parts of the body, all the way to the tips of our fingers and toes.

b. There are _____ kinds of fruit — apples, oranges, ba-nanas, and so forth.

14a. Breathing and digesting our food are called *autonomous functions*,

and they _____ whether or not we think about them.

b. It is difficult to drive in a snowstorm. Every time one

_____, the traffic moves very slowly.

Self-Test

Fill in each blank line with the correct word from the list below.

complicated	developed	function	message	various
consists	distinguish	impulse	occurs	volume
contain	form	located	primitive	

1. Many deaf people use sign language to talk to each other. Some peo-

ple think that sign languages are _____ languages. This is not true. Sign languages are completely developed languages.

2. It is simple to knit a sweater in only one color. It is more

_____ to knit a sweater in two or three different colors.

3. A two-liter bottle can contain a greater _____ of liquid than a one-liter bottle can.

4. A basket cannot _____ as a container for water. The water will run out of the basket.

5. A one-liter bottle cannot _____ as much liquid as a two-liter bottle can.

6. In this chapter, the word *primitive* is the opposite of _____.

7. Could you please tell me where the post office is _____?

8. I stood beside the swimming pool because I did not want to go in the

   water. Then someone bumped into me. The _____
   from the bump pushed me into the water.

9. Every time a thunderstorm _____, my dog hides under
   the bed.

10. My favorite meal _____ of boiled lobster and a large
    salad.

11. Most people cannot _____ Americans from Canadians.
    However, their accents are different.

12. Snowflakes _____ in many different shapes and
    patterns.

13. Mr. Jones isn't here now. Would you like to leave a _____
    for him?

14. People in the United States speak American English, but they have

    different accents in _____ parts of the country.

Synonyms

Below is a list of words followed by eight sentences. Each sentence contains one underlined word. The words in the list are **synonyms** for the underlined words in the sentences. That is, each word in the list has the same meaning as an underlined word in a sentence.
   Rewrite each sentence using the correct synonyms. The first one has been done for you.

adequate	different	happened	needed
certain	form	hold	size

1. On International Day at school, we were able to try new foods from
   various countries.

   On International Day at school, we were able to try new foods

   from different countries.

2. A one-liter bottle can <u>contain</u> a little more liquid than a one-quart bottle.

    _____

3. I saw the accident because I was looking out the window when it <u>occurred</u>.

    _____

4. A learner's permit is <u>required</u> before you can learn to drive a car.

    _____

5. A cube does not have the same <u>shape</u> as a sphere.

    _____

6. When she sets the table, my mother always folds the napkins in a <u>specific</u> way. She never folds them any other way.

    _____

7. A sweater will provide <u>sufficient</u> warmth today. It's not very cold.

    _____

8. A one-liter bottle is slightly larger in <u>volume</u> than a one-quart bottle.

    _____

Pronoun Reference/Substitution

In Chapter 1, we said that pronouns can refer to (or substitute for) groups of words.

> a. **The water was very cold yesterday.**
>
> b. **That** is why we didn't go swimming.

That in sentence **b** refers to all of sentence **a**.

> a. Many Americans have **dogs and cats** in their homes.
>
> b. **These animals** are like members of the family.

These animals in sentence **b** refers to **dogs and cats** in sentence **a**.

Below are some sentences from the reading selection. Each underlined pronoun refers to a group of words.
    Circle the letter of the correct answer. The first one is done for you.

1. The brain of a human being is only a small part of the human body, but it is an extremely important one.

    The word **it** refers to

    a. the brain of a human being.
    b. a small part.
    c. the human body.

2. The brains of primitive vertebrates such as fish, frogs, and snakes are much smaller than the human brain, and they are tube-like in shape.

    The word **they** refers to

    a. the human brain.
    b. fish, frogs, and snakes.
    c. the brains of primitive vertebrates.

3. Some examples of mammals are elephants, deer, dogs, mice, and people. They have brains that are somewhat different from the brains of primitive vertebrates.

   The word **they** refers to

      a. examples.
      b. elephants, deer, dogs, mice, and people.
      c. primitive vertebrates.

4. The human midbrain is small and folded inside the rest of the brain, so it is difficult to see.

   The word **it** refers to

      a. the human midbrain.
      b. the rest of the brain.
      c. folded inside.

5. These are at the bottom rear of the brain, near the place where it is attached to the spinal cord.

   The word **it** refers to

      a. the bottom rear.
      b. the brain.
      c. the place.

6. There are also a number of small glands located in the brain. The thalamus and hypothalamus are two of these.

   The word **these** refers to

      a. a number of small glands located in the brain.
      b. a number of small glands.
      c. the thalamus and hypothalamus.

7. The human brain is a computer (when it is computing, we are thinking.

   The word **it** refers to

      a. the human brain.
      b. the human brain is a computer.
      c. is computing.

8. Actions like running or picking something up require thinking. We do <u>these things</u> on purpose.

The words **these things** refer to

    a. actions.
    b. running or picking something up.
    c. thinking.

9. The brain and the nervous system also cause us to do things without thinking — such as breathing or digesting our food. We do not have to command our brains to do <u>these things</u>.

The words **these things** refer to

    a. the brain and the nervous system.
    b. without thinking.
    c. breathing or digesting our food.

10. We also do not have to command our hearts to beat because the brain and the nervous system do <u>it</u> for us.

The word **it** refers to

    a. command our hearts to beat.
    b. the brain.
    c. the nervous system.

Organization: Main Topics

Below is a list of the main topics of each paragraph in the reading. However, they are not in the correct order. Number them in the correct order. Put the number 1 on the line of the main topic of paragraph 1. Put the number 2 on the line in front of the main topic of paragraph 2, and so on. The first one has been done for you.

_____ Describes the brains of primitive vertebrates

_____ Describes parts of the human brain

_____ Concluding paragraph

_____ Describes how messages go through the nervous system

___1___ Introduction

_____ Discusses the brains of higher vertebrates (mammals)

_____ Compares the human brain to a computer, a switchboard, and a message center

_____ Discusses autonomous functions

Comprehension Questions

Answer the following questions by circling **True** or **False**. If a statement is false, explain why it is false.

Paragraph 1

   1. **True** or **False**   Scientists and engineers can build computers that are more powerful than the human brain.

   2. **True** or **False**   The human body contains a good deal of water.

Paragraph 2

   3. **True** or **False**   All vertebrates have the same-sized brain.

Paragraph 3

   4. **True** or **False**   Mammals are warm-blooded and nurse their young.

5. **True** or **False**   Elephants, deer, dogs, mice, and people have brains that are somewhat different from the brains of primitive vertebrates.

6. **True** or **False**   Human beings have an extremely large cerebrum.

Paragraph 4

7. **True** or **False**   The human midbrain is difficult to see.

8. **True** or **False**   René Descartes thought that the pineal gland was the place where the body was in contact with the soul.

9. **True** or **False**   The tuatara's third eye is able to distinguish light and darkness.

Paragraph 5

10. **True** or **False**   The human brain receives messages from our eyes, ears, nose, and tongue.

Paragraph 6

11. **True** or **False**   Each one of the 50 billion nerve cells in the brain is in touch with all the other 50 billion nerve cells.

12. **True** or **False**   We can pick something up because the brain sends a command through the nervous system to our muscles.

Paragraph 7

13. **True** or **False**   We have to think about autonomous functions.

✍ Writing Assignment: Summary

Remember, a summary is shorter than the original writing.

Step 1   Read paragraph 5 of the reading selection carefully.

Step 2   Read paragraph 5 a second time. This time, draw a line under any words or short groups of words that you think are important.

Step 3   On a separate piece of paper, write the words and groups of words that you underlined.

Step 4   Compare your list of words with that of a partner or in small groups. Make changes if you think they are necessary.

Step 5   Now close your book. Use your list of words to help you write a summary of paragraph 5.

Do the same with paragraphs 6 and 7.

Daruma, the founder of Zen Buddhism, challenged his disciple:
"Give me your mind, and I will give it peace."
Courtesy of Michael Heron ©*1982.*

5 The Mind and the Brain

Below are some statements about the brain and the mind. There are no right or wrong answers. Read each statement and decide if you agree with it or disagree with it. Draw a circle around **Agree** or **Disagree** for each statement.

1. The brain and the mind are the same.   Agree   Disagree

2. The brain has physical existence like the body.   Agree   Disagree

3. The mind has physical existence like the body.   Agree   Disagree

4. The mind does not exist.   Agree   Disagree

5. The mind is the result of what the brain does.   Agree   Disagree

6. We use our entire brain when we think or move.   Agree   Disagree

7. We only use part of the brain when we try to remember something.   Agree   Disagree

8. Removing a part of the brain causes permanent damage to the mind's functions.   Agree   Disagree

Now discuss your answers with your classmates.

READING SELECTION

The Mind and the Brain

any hundreds of years ago, there was a man called Daruma, who was the founder of Zen Buddhism. One day he sat in front of a blank wall and meditated. A disciple approached him and said, "I have searched for a long time and still my mind has no peace. Please give my mind peace."

(2) Daruma replied, "Give me your mind and I will give it peace."

(3) Daruma's answer illustrates a problem that humanity has been trying to solve for more than 2500 years: What and where is the mind? Our own minds are very real to us, and yet the mind does not seem to have a physical existence. That is, it cannot be located in space. What is the relationship between the mind and the body? Dualists (believers in two) believe that both the body and the mind exist. According to the dualists, the body is made of matter and exists in time and space, and the mind is not made of matter and exists outside of time and space. To the dualists, the body is like a machine that runs according to the laws of physics and chemistry, but the mind is not controlled by these laws. (One philosopher called the mind "the ghost in the machine.")

(4) Some philosophers called materialists say that only matter exists and that the mind is an illusion. Other philosophers called mentalists say that only mind exists and that matter is an illusion. One humorist summed up both these arguments by saying, "No matter, never mind."

(5) Many philosophers and scientists have tried to decide where the mind is located in the human body. Two Greek philosophers, Empedocles and Aristotle, said that it was in the heart. Another Greek, Hippocrates of Cos, said that it was in the brain. An early doctor, Galen, thought the mind was located in the fluid inside the brain. At the beginning of the nineteenth century, a subject called phrenology was popular. According to phrenology, different functions of the mind were located in different parts of the brain. Phrenologists also believed that the bumps on a person's head revealed things about the brain (and mind) of that person.

(6) Many modern scientists believe that the mind and the brain are connected, or that possibly the mind is the result of what the brain does. Modern scientists who study the nervous system (neurologists) believe also that a thin layer on top of the cerebrum (called the cerebral cortex) is responsible for thinking and consciousness. This cerebral cortex is a quar-

ter of an inch thick and holds three quarters of the brain's 50 billion neurons or nerve cells.

(7)   Although most of what we regard as thinking goes on in the cerebral cortex, the other parts of the brain have different functions to perform. For example, the limbic system, which is a part of the forebrain, is responsible for emotions and memory. The medulla oblongata and a neighboring organ, the pons, control breathing and heart rhythm. The cerebellum is involved with motor responses (movements).

(8)   Even within the cerebrum, different locations seem to be associated with different kinds of mental activity. Scientists have been investigating the different functions of the right and left cerebral hemispheres for some time. One way to study these functions is to inject a person with a chemical compound called deoxyglucose (or DG) that contains radioactive oxygen. This makes it possible to see what areas of the brain are being used at a particular time because the DG concentrates in the areas of the brain that are working then. Therefore, scientists can tell which parts of the brain are being used by measuring the amount of radioactivity in different parts of the brain. As a person goes from doing mental arithmetic to imagining he or she is walking down a street to describing the contents of his or her living room, different parts of the person's brain "light up" by becoming more radioactive.

(9)   Electric stimulation of the brain can also show that the brain has different areas. When one area of one person's brain was stimulated, he thought about the death of his father with feelings of sorrow and guilt. When another area of his brain was stimulated, he had happy thoughts about his girl friend.

(10)   Although brain areas appear to be specialized, large sections of the brain can be surgically removed without much permanent damage to the functioning of the mind of the individual. This would seem to show that the brain acts as a whole in many ways and that one part of the brain can take over the functioning of another part.

EXERCISES

Scanning Questions

Look back at the reading selection and find the answers to the following questions. Remember, answer only what is asked for. It is not always necessary to write complete sentences.

Paragraph 3

1. What is a problem that humanity has been trying to solve for more than 2500 years?

   _____

2. Who believe that both the mind and the body exist?

   _____

3. According to dualists, what is the body?

   _____

4. According to dualists, what is the mind?

   _____

5. To the dualists, is the mind controlled by the laws of physics and chemistry?

   _____

Paragraph 4

6. What do materialists say about the mind?

   _____

7. What do mentalists say about the mind?

_____

Paragraph 5

8. Where did the following people say that the mind was located?

    a. Empedocles and Aristotle _____

    b. Hippocrates _____

    c. Galen _____

9. What did phrenologists say about the mind?

_____

Paragraph 6

10. What do modern neurologists believe is responsible for thinking and conciousness?

_____

11. What is the cerebral cortex?

_____

Paragraph 8

12. How do scientists study the different functions of the right and left cerebral hemispheres?

_____

13. Why does injecting a person with DG make it possible to see which areas of the brain are being used at a particular time?

_____

14. **Cause:** The DG concentrates in the areas of the brain that are working (at a particular time)

    Result: _____

Paragraph 9

15. Besides using the chemical compound DG, what else can show that the brain has different areas?

_____

Vocabulary

Below are seven pairs of sentences. Sentence **a** of each pair is from the reading selection. Look back at the reading selection, if necessary, to find the correct word for sentence **a**. Write the word on the blank line in sentence **a**. Then read sentence **b** carefully. Write the word from sentence **a** on the blank line in sentence **b**. This word has the same meaning in both sentences.

approach(ed)   exist   matter (noun)   solve
control(led)   illusion   relationship

1a. A disciple _____ him and said, "I have searched for a long time, and still my mind has no peace."

  b. Mary is afraid of dogs, so she will not go near one. However, John

     likes dogs. When he saw a dog yesterday he _____ it and patted it.

2a. Daruma's answer illustrates a problem that humanity has been try-

     ing to _____ for 2500 years.

  b. I like to read mystery stories, but I can't _____ the mystery in them. I always have to read to the end of the book before I know who the murderer was. My friend, however, always knows the answer before the end.

3a. What is the _____ between the mind and the body?

   b. Your mother's sister is your aunt. That is her _____ to you.

4a. Dualists (believers in two) believe that both the body and the mind

   _____.

   b. Many little American children believe in Santa Claus. Later they

   learn that he does not really _____. It is their parents who give them the Christmas presents.

5a. According to the dualists, the body is made of _____ and exists in time and space.

   b. Things that we can see and touch are made of _____. Emotions such as happiness and sadness are not. We cannot see them or touch them.

6a. To the dualists, the body is like a machine that runs according to the laws of physics and chemistry, but the mind is not

   _____ by these laws.

   b. A car does not drive itself. A car is _____ by the driver.

7a. Some philosophers called materialists say that only matter exists,

   and that the mind is an _____.

   b. A magician seems to find money behind someone's ear, but it is

   only an _____. The money was in the magician's hand all the time.

Do the same with the following:

associate(d) (with)   involve(d)   specialized
concentrate(s)   responsible (for)   stimulation

8a. Modern scientists who study the nervous system (neurologists) believe also that a thin layer on top of the cerebrum (called the cere-

bral cortex) is _____ for thinking and consciousness.

b. Smoking is _____ for many deaths from lung cancer.

9a. The cerebellum is _____ with motor responses
(movements).

b. The president of a company is _____ with the overall
management of the company.

10a. Even within the cerebrum, different locations seem to be

_____ with different kinds of mental activity.

b. When my mother made spaghetti, there was always a smell of
garlic in the air. In my mind, the smell of garlic is always

_____ with my mother's spaghetti.

11a. This makes it possible to see what areas of the brain are being used

at a particular time because the DG _____ in the areas of the brain that are working then.

b. Students don't like to sit at the front of a classroom. They usually

_____ in the seats in the back of the room, so there
are only a few students in the front.

12a. Electric _____ of the brain can also show that the
brain has different areas.

b. I got a lot of _____ from Professor Smith's talk. I
learned a number of new ideas.

13a. Although brain areas appear to be _____, large sections of the brain can be surgically removed without much permanent damage to the functioning of the mind of the individual.

b. The Giant Panda has very _____ eating habits. It will eat only one type of food. That one type of food is the bamboo tree.

Self-Test

Fill in the blank lines with the correct word from the list below.

approach	controls	involved	responsible
associated	existed	matter	solve
concentrates	illusion	relationship	specialized
			stimulation

1. When the full moon is rising, it looks larger than usual. This is an

   _____. When the moon gets higher in the sky, we see it as its normal size.

2. A computer cannot do anything by itself. The user _____ the computer.

3. There were dinosaurs on the earth millions of years before human

   beings _____.

4. John is very good at mathematics. He can _____ very complicated math problems.

5. American university students sometimes have a friendly

   _____ with their professors.

6. A chair is made of _____. An idea is not.

7. The engine of a car is _____ for making the car move.

8. When adults can't have something that they want, they do not cry and yell. Crying and yelling for something is behavior that is

    _____ with children, not adults.

9. When you mix oil and water in a glass, they do not stay mixed. The water sinks to the bottom of the glass, and the oil

    _____ on top.

10. Mr. Jones makes furniture. He has many different tools for this.

    Each tool is _____ for a particular function. He can't use one tool for two different functions.

11. Your grades in your classes are _____ with the amount of studying that you do.

12. My little daughter is very shy. When strangers _____ her, she runs away.

13. Some people take a cold shower in the morning. The _____ of the cold water wakes them up fast.

Ellipsis

In speaking and writing English, we often do not repeat words. Sometimes we replace words with pronouns.

▶ *Example*

> My neighbor's dog is noisy. It barks a lot.

But sometimes we **omit** words. This means that we do not replace words with pronouns. We just do not repeat them.

▶ *Example*

    a. Yesterday was a nice sunny day.
    b. Today is not.

The words that are not repeated in sentence **b** are "a nice sunny day." Sentence **b** really means: Today is not a nice sunny day.

In the sentences below, some words are not repeated. On the blank lines, write the word or words that are not repeated. The first one is done for you.

  1. Mary can swim, but John can't.

                                  swim

  2. John has three sisters, and Mary has two.

  3. There are many different kinds of lettuce. My favorite is romaine.

4. I am the youngest student in the class, and John is the oldest.

   _____

5. Mary doesn't know how to type, but she wants to learn.

   _____

6. John can speak two languages. His friend can speak three.

   _____

7. Cats climb trees, but dogs don't.

   _____

8. She can type 80 words per minute, and I can type 60.

   _____

The sentences below are from the reading selections. Read them and answer the questions.

1. However, most people no longer think that this is a good explanation for the pork taboo. Another explanation is that the Israelites were nomads — they were always moving from place to place.

   "The Israelites were nomads" — what is this another explanation for?

   _____

2. There seem to be three kinds of cannibalism. There is the kind that happens when a group of people is isolated from other people and has no other source of food.

   In the second sentence above, what words are not repeated after "kind"?

   _____

3. This would seem to show that the brain acts as a whole in many ways and that one part of the brain can take over the functioning of another part.

   What can one part of the brain do for another part of the brain?

   _____

4. For example, if our right hand is injured, we can learn to write with our left.

   Can we learn to write with our left hand if our right hand is injured?

   _____

Organization: Mapping Topics and Details

The following sentence is from paragraph 3 of the reading selection. It is a topic sentence.

**Dualists (believers in two) believe that both the
body and the mind exist.**

The next two sentences of paragraph 3 give details about the dualists' beliefs. Some are beliefs about the body, and some are beliefs about the mind.

These details are listed below.

✔ ■ is made of matter
  ■ is not made of matter
  ■ exists in time and space
  ■ exists outside of time and space
  ■ runs according to the laws of physics and chemistry
  ■ is not controlled by the laws of physics and chemistry

Write each detail above in the correct box on the map. The first one is done for you.

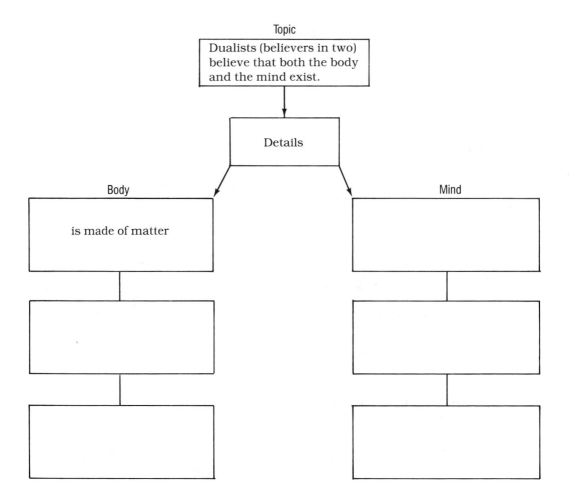

Below are the main topic and the details from paragraph 7 of the reading selection. Fill in the boxes of the map on page 97 with the correct information.

- The other parts of the brain have different functions to perform.
- limbic system
- medulla oblongata and pons
- cerebellum
- responsible for emotions and memory
- control breathing and heart rhythms
- involved with motor responses (movements)

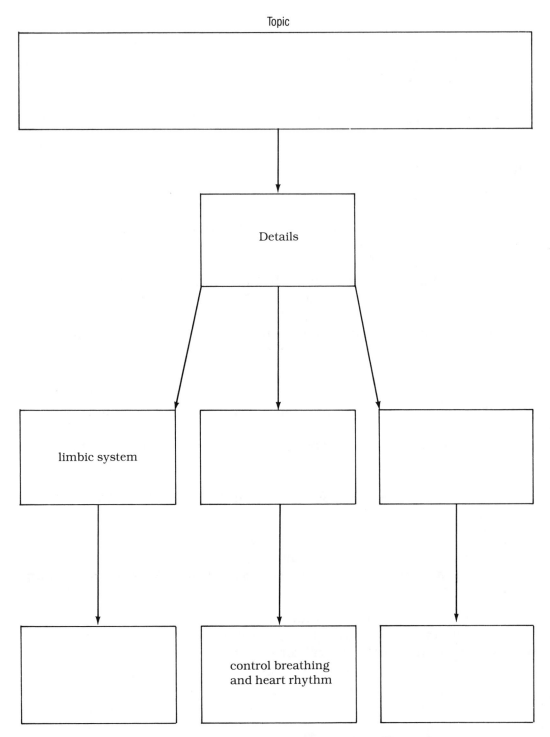

Working with a partner, make your own map for paragraph 8. Begin with the main topic.

Comprehension Questions

Answer the following questions by circling **True** or **False**. If a statement is false, explain why it is false.

Paragraphs 1–4

1. **True** or **False**   Daruma gave the disciple peace of mind.

2. **True** or **False**   Humanity has solved the problem of "What is the mind?"

3. **True** or **False**   Something that has a physical existence can be located in space.

4. **True** or **False**   Materialists and mentalists say the same thing about matter.

Paragraph 6

5. **True** or **False**   Modern scientists know what the mind is.

6. **True** or **False**   The cerebral cortex is a thin layer on top of the cerebrum.

To answer the next two questions, draw a circle around the letter of the correct answer.

Paragraph 7

7. **Line 3**   The words "for example" mean that this sentence and the next two sentences are examples of something. What are they examples of?

   a. what we regard as thinking
   b. different functions of other parts of the brain
   c. functions of the cerebral cortex

Paragraph 8

8. Line 4   The words "these functions" refer to

   a. the different functions of the right cerebral hemisphere.
   b. the different functions of the left cerebral hemisphere.
   c. the different functions of the right and left cerebral hemispheres.

9. True or **False**   Injecting a person with DG makes it possible to see what areas of the brain are being used at a particular time.

Write the answer on the blank line.

10. What does measuring the amount of radioactivity in different parts of the brain tell a scientist?

_____

✍ Writing Assignment: Opinion

Look back at your choices in the Pre-Reading Discussion on page 83. Do you have different opinions now, or do you still feel the same way? Why?

Write a short paragraph that gives your opinion about the mind and the brain. Tell why you believe the way that you do.

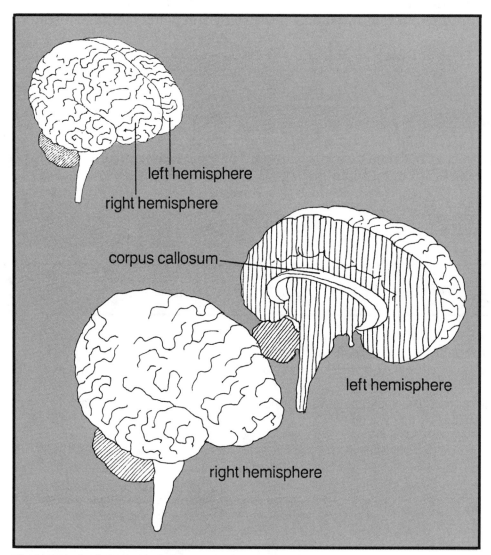

left hemisphere

right hemisphere

corpus callosum

left hemisphere

right hemisphere

The brain is divided into two halves, each of which controls the opposite side of the body. *Reprinted with the permission of Houghton-Mifflin Co., from* The Amazing Brain, *by Robert Ornstein and Richard F. Thompson. Illustration by David Macaulay.*

6 Right Brain, Left Brain

PRE-READING DISCUSSION

In small groups, discuss the following:

The title of the reading selection in this chapter is "Right Brain, Left Brain."

- Why do we have two sides to our brains?
- Is it possible that each side has different functions?
- What do you think each side of the brain is responsible for?

Make a list under each heading below. Some functions are music, speech, reading, and mathematics. Add any others that you can think of.

Left Brain	Right Brain

- What kinds of things can happen to someone when an area of the brain is injured (hurt)?

READING SELECTION

Right Brain, Left Brain

I n studying the brain, scientists have tried to learn what parts of the brain correspond to what kinds of activity in our bodies. They would like to be able to draw a map that shows how every small part of the brain corresponds to some specific activity (vision in the left eye, for example) or to some specific memory. We now feel that this is impossible. The brain and the way it works is too complex to describe in such a simple way. Besides that, if different parts of the brain are injured, other parts of the brain can take over for the injured parts. The body is the same way. For example, if our right hand is injured, we can learn to write with our left. In addition, people who cannot use either of their hands have learned to write with their feet or with pencils in their mouths.

(2)   You learned in a previous reading that thinking and much of the conscious work of the brain is done by the cerebral hemispheres. The left cerebral hemisphere controls the right side of the body: the right eye, right arm, right hand, right leg and so on. In the same way, the right hemisphere controls the left side of the body.

(3)   We have gotten much of our knowledge about how different parts of the brain work from studying people with injured brains. *Aphasia* is a word that describes an injury that impairs (or hurts) a person's ability to use language. Injuries to different parts of the brain produce different kinds of aphasia. Injury to an area called Broca's area in the frontal region of the left hemisphere produces a speech impairment known as Broca's aphasia. Someone with Broca's aphasia has great difficulty speaking but is able to understand speech and to read and write without difficulty.

(4)   Wernicke's aphasia occurs when another area of the brain, located in the left temporal region, is injured. Those with Wernicke's aphasia do not comprehend speech well and their reading and writing abilities are impaired. They are able to speak many words, but they often do not make sense.

(5)   One of the earliest discoveries about the areas of the brain was made more than a hundred years ago, in the middle third of the nineteenth century. This discovery was made by a number of scientists including one named Broca — the same man for whom Broca's area of the brain is named. He and others found that injuries to the left cerebral hemisphere

were much more likely to cause problems with language than injuries to the right cerebral hemisphere.

(6)   Most people are right handed, which means that they do most things with their right hand. We say that for these people the right hand is *dominant*. Because the left hemisphere controls both language and the right or dominant side of the body, people began to think that the left hemisphere was the dominant hemisphere and that the right hemisphere was not very intelligent. It is true that when things are seen by the left eye or picked up by the left hand the activity has to go through the right hemisphere, but the right hemisphere was pictured as only a sort of relay station and not as an equal partner to the left hemisphere.

(7)   For the first half of the twentieth century, this view of left hemisphere dominance was popular. We were seen as functioning with only half a brain (the left brain). According to this view, the right brain was greatly underused. Then, in the 1960s some operations were performed on epileptic patients that completely changed our thinking.

(8)   Epilepsy is a disease of the brain in which the patients have seizures or "fits," violent movements of the body over which they have no control and which they may not be aware of. These seizures are the result of abnormal electrical activity within the brain. Usually this abnormal activity is limited to one hemisphere, and epilepsy of this kind can often be controlled by medicine. But occasionally the electrical activity jumps across the corpus callosum to the other hemisphere. This produces an extremely violent seizure that cannot be controlled by medicine. In the 1960s, doctors tried to control the seizures of such patients by cutting the corpus callosum so that there was no connection between the two hemispheres of the brain.

(9)   Patients who had this operation performed on them functioned quite well in day-to-day life but showed some unusual behavior in the laboratory. They could say the name of an object that they held in their right hands, but they could not name an object held in the left hand (and therefore not "connected" to the left hemisphere). A picture of a naked person shown to the right eye caused one patient to giggle and blush, but the patient could not name or describe in words what she saw.

(10) A number of experiments showed that verbal and logical thinking activities were controlled by the left hemisphere and that spatial activities (for example, drawing) and music were controlled by the right hemisphere. The experimenters decided that creative activities in general were controlled by the right hemisphere.

(11) Investigators found these discoveries exciting, and, as is often the case, exaggerated claims were made. The belief was that everyone was dominated by either one or the other of the two hemispheres. Right-

brained people were imaginative and artistic. Left-brained people were logical, verbal, and mathematical. Then some people said that our system of education had always been better for left-brained people and that we should train the more imaginative and artistic people ("right-brained") by teaching to the right brain, although no one was sure how to do this.

(12) After a few years of excitement over these ideas, most investigators now agree with the idea that people had before Broca introduced his idea of hemispheric dominance. That is, that the brain is a whole and the right and left hemispheres work together. We don't use just half of our brain, nor do we use two separate brains. We use one whole brain, and this whole brain works extremely well.

EXERCISES

Scanning Questions

Look back at the reading selection to find the answers to the following questions. Work as quickly as you can.

Paragraph 1

1. What is too complex to describe in a simple way?

   _____

2. What happens when parts of the brain are injured?

   _____

3. What happens if someone's right hand is injured?

   _____

4. What have people who cannot use either of their hands learned to do?

_____

Paragraph 5

5. Which cerebral hemisphere controls the right side of the body?

_____

6. Which cerebral hemisphere controls the left side of the body?

_____

Paragraph 3

7. How have we gotten much of our knowledge about how different parts of the brain work?

_____

8. What is aphasia?

_____

9. What produces different kinds of aphasia?

_____

Paragraph 5

10. What is likely to cause problems with language?

_____

Paragraph 6

11. When you see something with your left eye, which hemisphere does that activity go through?

_____

Paragraph 7

12. In the 1960s, what were performed that completely changed our thinking?

_____

Paragraph 8

13. What are seizures the result of?

_____

14. What happens when the electrical activity jumps across the corpus callosum to the other hemisphere?

_____

15. In the 1960s, how did doctors try to control the seizures of such patients?

_____

Paragraph 9

16. What could patients who had this operation say about an object that they held in their right hand?

_____

17. Could these patients say the same thing about an object held in their left hand?

_____

Paragraph 10

18. What did a number of experiments show about verbal and logical thinking activities?

_____

19. What kind of activities did these experiments show were controlled by the right hemisphere?

_____

Vocabulary

Fill in the blank spaces with the correct words from the list below. Remember, sentence **a** of each pair is from the reading. Sentence **b** uses the same word as sentence **a** with the same meaning.

activity/activities	conscious	impair(s), (-ed)	produce
complex	correspond(s)	previous	

1a. In studying the brain, scientists have tried to learn what parts of the

brain _____ to what kinds of activity in our bodies.

b. If the signal light is green, I can go. If the signal light is red, I must

stop the car. Green _____ to *go* and red

_____ to *stop*.

2a. In studying the brain, scientists have tried to learn what parts of the

brain correspond to what kinds of _____ in our
bodies.

b. Reading and writing are two kinds of _____ we learn
in school.

3a. The brain and the way it works is too _____ to describe in such a simple way.

b. The engine of an automobile has many different parts that are arranged so that they all work together. The engine is very

_____ .

4a. You learned in a _____ reading that thinking and much of the conscious work of the brain is done by the cerebral hemispheres.

b. Typewriters were invented before computers. Typewriters were

_____ to computers.

5a. You learned in a previous reading that thinking and much of the

_____ work of the brain is done by the cerebral hemi sphere.

b. Picking something up is a _____ act. Digesting food is not. We do not have to think about digesting our food.

6a. *Aphasia* is a word that describes an injury that _____ (or hurts) a person's ability to use language.

b. After the automobile accident, John had to use a cane to walk. The

accident _____ his legs so he could not walk without a cane.

7a. Injuries to different parts of the brain _____ different kinds of aphasia.

b. Areas of the world that have lots of snow for most of the year seem

to _____ wild animals that have white fur. There are no wild animals with white fur in areas of the world that do not get much snow.

Do the same with the following:

> abnormalcreative   likely   view
> area   imaginative   limit(ed)

8a. Injury to an _____ called Broca's _____ in the frontal region of the left hemisphere produces a speech impairment known as Broca's aphasia.

  b. The kitchen is an _____ of the house used for preparing food.

9a. He and others found that injuries to the left cerebral hemisphere

were much more _____ to cause problems with language than injuries to the right cerebral hemisphere.

  b. Tomorrow afternoon I will either watch TV or play soccer. If it is a

nice day tomorrow, it is more _____ that I will play soccer.

10a. For the first half of the twentieth century, this _____ of the left hemisphere dominance was popular.

  b. Many people used to think that whales were fish, but the great sci-

entist Carl Linne took a different _____. He thought that they were warm-blooded mammals.

11a. These seizures are the result of _____ electrical activity within the brain.

  b. He always takes a shower in the morning. That is the normal thing

for him to do. Not to take a shower would be _____ for him.

12a. Usually this abnormal activity is _____ to one hemisphere.

   b. A ship can only move on water. Its ability to move is

   _____ to water.

13a. The experimenters decided that _____ activities in general were controlled by the right hemisphere.

   b. Writing a poem or a story is a _____ activity.

14a. Right-brained people were _____ and artistic.

   b. An _____ person thinks of new and different ways of doing something.

Self-Test

Fill in the blank lines with the correct words from the list below.

abnormal	complex	creative	likely	produce
activity	conscious	imaginative	limited	view
area	correspond	impairs	previous	

1. I spent the day _____ to the exam studying, so I did well on the exam.

2. Seventy percent of the earth's _____ is covered by water.

3. Drinking alcohol _____ your ability to drive a car.

4. Blinking our eyes is not usually a _____ activity.

5. Although a TV set looks simple on the outside, it is very

   _____ on the inside.

6. Playing chess is an _____ that doesn't interest me. I would rather play soccer.

7. Some birds seem to be able to talk. They are able to _____ a few words such as "hello" and "goodbye."

8. Fish swim through water the way that birds fly through the air. For a fish, water _____ to air.

9. He does not like to read or take a walk or play games. He only likes to watch TV. His likes are very _____.

10. Sometimes a cow is born with two heads, but this is _____.

11. My mother used to make up stories to tell us before we went to sleep. She was very _____.

12. The sky is getting very dark. It is _____ to rain soon.

13. Mary makes all her own clothes. She is very _____.

14. In my _____, it is very important to eat a healthy diet. Other people think that exercise is the most important thing.

Substitution: one, then, there, so

In previous chapters, there were exercises on pronoun reference/substitution. In those exercises, you substituted pronouns for nouns or noun phrases (such as *baby birds* and *long, sloping foreheads*).

We can also use the words **one**, **there**, **then**, and **so** as substitutes for other words or groups of words (phrases).

one, then, there

one substitutes for nouns and noun phrases
then substitutes for time expressions
there substitutes for place expressions

Read the following paragraphs.

Draw a circle around the words **one, then,** and **there.**

Then draw a circle around each of the words or phrases that **one, then,** and **there** refer to.

Draw an arrow that connects the substitute word to the word or phrase that it substitutes for. The first one has been done for you.

The city of Chicago has many different kinds of museums. The Museum of Science and Industry is a good one for children because they can touch things there. At Christmas time, the Museum of Science and Industry has an exhibit of Christmas trees from all over the world. Each one is decorated differently. Many people go there then to see the Christmas trees. They are very beautiful.

My favorite museum is the Art Institute. I like to go there and look at the pictures. They are like old friends. The Art Institute has two restaurants. There is an inside restaurant, and in the summer, there is also an outside restaurant. The outside one is open only in the summer. People like to eat outside then.

so   **so** is used together with an auxiliary verb such as **do, can, is, was,** and so forth to show that two things are the same.

John likes coffee. **So** do I. (I like coffee.)

The Museum of Science and Industry is a very interesting museum. **So** is the Field Museum. (The Field Museum is a very interesting museum.)

Below are some sentences from previous chapters in this book. Read the sentences and answer the questions.

1. No one in India will kill or eat the sacred cows. It is taboo to do so.

   What is it taboo to do in India?

   _____

2. The brain of a human being is only a small part of the human body, but it is an extremely important one.

What is an extremely important part of the human body?

_____

3. This discovery was made by a number of scientists, including one named Broca.

Was Broca a scientist? _____

Signal Words

such as   **such as** signals an example or examples.

There are many different types of automobiles, such as Hondas, Volkswagens, Toyotas, and Fords.

In the above sentence, Hondas, Volkswagens, Toyotas, and Fords are examples of different types of automobiles.

Read the following sentences and answer the questions.

1. All human beings have certain basic needs, such as eating, drinking, and keeping warm and dry.

What are three examples of basic human needs?

_____

2. The brains of primitive vertebrates such as fish, frogs, and snakes are much smaller than the human brain, and they are tube-like in shape.

What are three examples of primitive vertebrates?

_____

True or **False**   The brains of fish, frogs, and snakes are tube-like in shape.

3. The brain and the nervous system also cause us to do some things without thinking — such as breathing or digesting our food.

What are two examples of things that the brain causes us to do without thinking?

_____

in addition, These words signal additional information or ideas.
also

      a. I like to swim.
      b. I also like to ski.

The word also in sentence **b** signals that this sentence gives additional information about things that I like to do.

      c. In order to learn a new language, you must study the grammar of that language.
      d. In addition, you must practice speaking it.

Sentences **c** and **d** tell two things you must do in order to learn a new language.

Read the following sentences and and answer the questions.

1. We all have ideas about what kinds of foods are good to eat. We also have ideas about what kinds of foods are bad to eat.

What two ideas do we have about foods?

_____

2. Another example is that Americans do not eat dogs. In the United States dogs are very important to people as pets. In addition, dogs have value as protection against criminals.

What are two reasons that Americans do not eat dogs?

_____

_____

3. If one part of the body is injured, other parts of the body can take over for the injured parts. For example, if our right hand is injured, we can learn to write with our left. In addition, people who cannot use either of their hands have learned to write with their feet or with pencils in their mouths.

What are three parts of the body that can take over for other parts of the body?

_____

that is   **that is** signals an explanation of the previous statement.

   a. **For a spider, spinning a web is instinctive.**
   b. **That is, a spider does not have to learn how to spin a web. It knows how to do it when it is born.**

   Sentence **b** explains what <u>instinctive</u> means — behavior that does not have to be learned.

Read the following sentences and answer the questions:

1. The mind does not seem to have a physical existence. That is, it cannot be located in space.

What is a way of explaining something that *has* a physical existence?

_____

2. Most investigators now agree with the idea that people had before Broca introduced his idea of hemispheric dominance. That is, that the brain is a whole and the left and right hemispheres work together.

What is the idea that people had before Broca introduced his idea of hemispheric dominance?

_____

SIGNAL WORDS

Example	Contrast/Unexpected Information	Additional Information
for example such as e.g.	but although however	also in addition furthermore

Cause/Reason	Result/Effect	Explanation
because	so therefore as a result thus	that is i.e.

Word Families

Listed below are different forms of some of the vocabulary words in Chapters 4, 5, and 6. The new forms are different parts of speech. Study them before doing the exercise.

Verbs	Nouns	Adjectives	Adverbs
complete	completion	complete/incomplete	completely
——	——	conscious/unconscious	consciously/ unconsciously
create	creation	creative	creatively
illustrate	illustration	illustrated	——
injure	injury/injuries	injured/uninjured	——
limit	limitation	limited/unlimited	——
produce	production	productive/unproductive	——

1.   complete   completion   complete/incomplete   completely

    a. I am making a sweater for my sister's birthday. Her birthday is in

      two weeks, but the sweater is still _____.

b. I hope I can _____ it before her birthday.

c. People used to think that the earth was flat. That idea was

_____ wrong.

d. I want to own all the books by that writer. She has written fifteen books, but I have only ten of them. My collection of her books is

not _____.

e. We won't get our grades for this class until the

_____ of the semester.

2.   conscious/unconscious   consciously/unconsciously

a. When a good typist types, her fingers move _____.
She does not have to think about where to put her fingers.

b. Breathing is an _____ activity.

c. You do the exercises in this book _____. You must think about them when you do them.

d. Doing the exercises in this book is a _____ activity.

3.   create   creation   creative   creatively

a. I don't use other people's patterns when I make a sweater. I

_____ my own patterns.

b. In order to create a new pattern, I must think _____.

c. My friend tries to make new patterns, but she can't. She is not

very _____.

d. The _____ of something new makes me happy.

4.   illustrate   illustrations   illustrated

   a. This book has pictures in it. It is an _____ book.

   b. She drew pictures to _____ her meaning.

   c. The _____ in this book correspond to the topics of the readings.

5.   injure   injuries   injured/uninjured

   a. Two cars were involved in an accident. Everyone in the first car was all right. No one in that car was _____.

   b. In the second car, three people had _____ and one person did not. That is, one person was _____.

   c. Automobile accidents can _____ people.

6.   limit   limitations   limited/unlimited

   a. My doctor told me to _____ the amount of sweet and fat foods that I eat.

   b. I am not happy with the _____ on my eating.

   c. I would like to eat an _____ amount of sweet foods!

   d. I want to eat only a _____ amount of healthy foods!

7.   produce   production   productive/unproductive

   a. The _____ of grammatical sentences in a language depends on knowing the grammar rules.

   b. All languages use a limited number of grammar rules to _____ an unlimited number of grammatical sentences.

c. We can grow flowers in good dirt. Good dirt is very

_____ for growing flowers.

d. Most flowers do not grow well in sand. Sand is

_____ for growing flowers.

Comprehension Questions

Answer the following questions by circling **True** or **False**, by circling the letter of the correct answer, or by writing the answer on the blank line. If a statement is false, explain why it is false.

Paragraph 1

1. **True** or **False**   If different parts of the body are injured, other parts of the body can take over for the injured parts.

Paragraph 2

2. **True** or **False**   The right side of the brain controls the right eye, right arm, right hand, and right leg.

Paragraph 3

3. Broca's aphasia is different from Wernicke's aphasia in which way?

   a. Someone with Broca's aphasia can speak, but someone with Wernicke's aphasia cannot.
   b. Someone with Broca's aphasia can understand speech and read and write without difficulty, but someone with Wernicke's aphasia cannot.
   c. Broca's aphasia comes from an injury to the left side of the brain, and Wernicke's aphasia comes from an injury to the right side of the brain.

Paragraph 5

4. **True** or **False**   One of the earliest discoveries about the areas of the brain was that injuries to the left area of the brain were more likely to cause problems with language than injuries to the right area of the brain.

Paragraph 6

5. **Cause:** The left hemisphere controls both language and the right or dominant side of the body.

   Result: _____

   _____

Paragraph 7

6. **True** or **False**   Ideas about the left brain and the right brain changed in the 1960s.

Paragraph 8

7. **True** or **False**   When the electrical activity of epilepsy jumps across the corpus callosum, the seizures can be controlled by medicine.

8. **True** or **False**   When the corpus callosum is cut, the two hemispheres of the brain are not connected.

Paragraph 10

9. **True** or **False**   Drawing is an example of a spatial activity.

Paragraph 11

10. **True** or **False**   People knew how to teach to the right brain.

Paragraph 12

11. **True** or **False**   Investigators now agree that the right brain and the left brain work separately.

✍ Writing Assignment

Read each paragraph again and write one question for each paragraph.

After you write your questions, find a partner. Ask each other the questions that you wrote.

Look at the reading selection to find the answers to your partner's questions. Answer the questions orally. Do not write the answers.

Courtesy of South African Airways.

7 Rebirth and Karma

In small groups, discuss the following.

In the past, different cultures have buried their dead with such things as food, cooking pots, jewelry, and little figures of people.
Why did they do this?

What do you know about the following words? Use your dictionary to help you.

karma   **reincarnation**   **rebirth**   **nirvana**

Courtesy of U.S. Department of Agriculture.

An ancient Hindu belief states that criminals are reborn in the bodies of animals. Do you see anyone you know here?

READING SELECTION

Rebirth and Karma

Many people believe that the life of an individual man or woman goes on even after the death of the body. Even 60,000 years ago, our distant ancestors were burying their dead with food and tools. They probably did this because they thought that the dead person could use the food and tools in another world. The ancient Egyptians took a great deal of trouble to preserve the bodies of dead people because they believed that they would live again. Today, the major religions still believe in some sort of life after death.

(2)   Today, there are two principal beliefs concerning a life after death. The three religions that originated in the Middle East — Judaism, Christianity, and Islam — believe that we have one life here followed by one life after death. The two religions that originated in India — Hinduism and Buddhism — believe that we have a succession of different lives. Each life is spent in a different body. After we "die" in one body, we will be born again in a different body. This belief in a succession of lives in different bodies is often called reincarnation or rebirth.

(3)   Many of those who believe in rebirth believe that we were not human beings in all of our past lives. In some of them we might have been gods or supernatural beings. In some, on the other hand, we might have been animals. Not harming or eating animals is sometimes part of the ethics of believers in rebirth. This is because the souls or minds of animals might have been in human bodies at one time.

(4)   Believers in rebirth see life as an endless succession of lives in different bodies. They do not think this cycle of rebirth ever had a beginning. However, both Hindus and Buddhists believe it is possible for this process to have an end. They regard it as desirable to escape from this endless process of birth and death, which they call *sansara*. The escape from *sansara* is to a state called *nirvana*. This state is difficult to describe but seems to be a state of pure consciousness free from the material world. Buddhists believe that when the Buddha died he attained *nirvana* rather than being born in another body.

(5)   Tibetan Buddhists believe that when the body dies the soul or self goes to an in-between region called the *Bardo* before being born again. The stay in the Bardo may last as long as forty-nine days. There are three stages in the Bardo. In the first, the person is aware of a clear pure light.

This stage provides an opportunity for people to free themselves from life-and-death and attain a *nirvana*-like state. Eventually this light fades and the person passes on to the next stage, in which he or she is met by a number of supernatural beings. Finally, in the third stage, the person moves towards the womb in which he or she is to be reborn.

(6)   *Karma* is another belief that is also closely connected to rebirth. Believers in karma believe that doing good or bad actions results in our accumulating good or bad karma. This karma works itself out in our lives and may appear in the form of good fortune or bad fortune. Karma may also carry over from one life to the next. A person who has done many good deeds in one life may be born as a rich and happy person in the next life. On the other hand, a person who has done many bad deeds will pay for them in his or her next life.

(7)   An ancient Hindu book called *The Laws of Manu* says that people who commit various crimes will be born in the bodies of animals in their next lives. A person who steals grain is reborn as a rat, for example. If he steals honey, he is reborn as a bee, and so forth. There are many stories of the previous lives of the Buddha. In a number of them, he is an elephant, which is regarded as a noble animal. However, although the elephant is noble, it is best to be reborn as a human being because it is only as a human being that one can attain nirvana.

(8)   Believers in rebirth sometimes also believe in heavens or hells. Unlike the Christian heaven or hell, however, these are not permanent. They are places where people stay while enjoying the rewards of their good karma or being punished for their bad karma. When their karma is used up, they are born again. Through the accumulation of good karma a person may be born in more and more favorable lives. The better their karma, the more likely it is that people can gain *nirvana* or can escape from the continual cycle of birth-and-death known as *sansara*.

EXERCISES

Scanning Questions

Look back at the reading to find the answers to the following questions. Remember, answer only what is asked for.

Paragraph 1

1. Why did our distant ancestors bury their dead with food and tools?

   _____

2. Why did the ancient Egyptians take a great deal of trouble to preserve the bodies of dead people?

   _____

3. What do the major religions still believe in today?

   _____

Paragraph 2

4. What are the three religions that originated in the Middle East?

   _____

5. What do they believe about life after death?

   _____

6. What are the two religions that originated in India?

   _____

7. What do they believe about life after death?

   _____

8. What is the belief in a succession of lives in different bodies called?

   _____

Paragraph 3

9. According to those who believe in rebirth, what are some things we might have been in our past lives?

   _____

Paragraph 4

10. Who does not think that the process of rebirth ever had a beginning?

    _____

11. Who believe that it is possible for the process of rebirth to have an end?

    _____

12. What does _nirvana_ seem to be?

    _____

Paragraph 5

13. Where do Tibetan Buddhists believe that the soul goes when the body dies?

    _____

14. What happens in the third stage of the Bardo?

    _____

Paragraph 6

15. What do believers in karma believe?

_____

16. In what form may karma appear?

_____

17. What may happen to a person who has done many good deeds in one life?

_____

Paragraph 7

18. According to the book called *The Laws of Manu*, what happens to a person who steals grain?

_____

19. What happens to a person who steals honey?

_____

Paragraph 8

20. To believers in rebirth, what are heavens and hells?

_____

Vocabulary

Fill in the blanks with the correct words from the list below. Sentence **a** of each pair of sentences is from the reading. Sentence **b** of each pair uses the same word with the same meaning as in Sentence **a**.

cycle	originate(d)	principal	succession
escape(d)	preserve	region	

1a. The ancient Egyptians took a great of trouble to

_____ the bodies of dead people because they believed that they would live again.

b. Once I caught a beautiful butterfly. I wanted to keep it as long as I

could, so I put it in a glass box to _____ it.

2a. Today, there are two _____ beliefs concerning a life after death.

b. The United States has two _____ political parties: the Democratic and the Republican. It also has a number of smaller political parties.

3a. The three religions that _____ in the Middle East — Judaism, Christianity, and Islam — believe that we have one life here followed by one life after death.

b. Most people believe that North American Indians

_____ in Asia and migrated to North America.

4a. The two religions that originated in India — Hinduism and Buddhism — believe that we have a _____ of different lives.

b. A _____ of unfortunate events prevented him from getting to work on time. First, he could not find his car keys. Then his car would not start. After that, he missed the bus and had to walk.

5a. They do not think this _____ of rebirth ever had a beginning.

b. A day and a night make one _____ of light and darkness.

6a. They regard it as desirable to _____ from this endless process of birth and death, which they call *sansara*.

b. The prisoner _____ from jail, but the police captured him and returned him to jail.

7a. Tibetan Buddhists believe that when the body dies, the soul or self

goes to an in-between _____ called the Bardo before being born again.

b. The Midwest is the _____ of the United States in which the Great Lakes are located.

Do the same with the following:

accumulate/ing	commit(ted)	opportunity	reward(s)
appear(s)	fade(s)	punish(ed)	

8a. This stage provides an _____ for people to free themselves from life-and-death and attain a *nirvana*-like state.

b. Free education gives everyone an _____ to learn.

9a. Eventually this light _____ and the person passes on to the next stage, in which he or she is met by a number of supernatural beings.

b. Bright colors _____ in strong sunlight. That is, when a bright-colored cloth is exposed to sunlight a lot, the color gradually becomes less bright.

10a. Believers in karma believe that doing good or bad actions results in

our _____ good or bad karma.

  b. The snow was falling rapidly. It was coming down so fast that two or

three inches were _____ each hour.

11a. This karma works itself out in our lives and may

_____ in the form of good fortune or bad fortune.

  b. After the rain stops, the clouds go away and the sun

_____ again.

12a. An ancient Hindu book called *The Laws of Manu* says that people

who _____ various crimes will be born in the bodies
of animals in their next lives.

  b. She _____ an error when she trusted him. He stole
some money from her.

13a. They are places where people stay while enjoying the

_____ of their good karma or being punished for their
bad karma.

  b. The police offered a _____ to anyone who could give
them information about the escaped thief. The amount was
$5,000.

14a. They are places where people stay while enjoying the rewards of

their good karma or being _____ for their bad karma.

  b. The little girl broke her mother's favorite glass bowl, so her mother

_____ her by making her stay inside all day.

Self-Test

Fill in the blank spaces with the correct words from the list below.

accumulate	cycle	opportunity	principal
appear	escaped	originated	regions
commit	fades	preserves	succession

1. The police left the room for a few minutes. This gave the thief an

    _____ to escape.

2. The four seasons form a _____. We have winter, spring, summer, fall, and then it is winter again.

3. Once I had a bird that I kept in a cage. Unfortunately, one day I left

    the cage door open, and the bird _____.

4. Most scientists believe that the first human ancestors

    _____ in Africa.

5. The various types of flowers in my garden grow in

    _____. The first ones appear in early spring. Others bloom in late spring. Later, the summer flowers appear.

6. The _____ cause of lung cancer is smoking.

7. Putting food in cans or jars _____ it for a long time.

8. Deserts are _____ of the world where there is very little rain.

9. If you keep money in a bank, it will _____ interest, and you will have more money.

10. He looked angry enough to _____ murder!

11. As night approaches, the daylight _____, and it gets darker.

12. When it gets dark, the stars _____ in the night sky.

Prediction: Signal Words

Circle the letter of the answer that will best complete each of the following according to the signal word.

⟹ *Example*

Mary usually takes the bus to school, but

a. she took the bus today.
b. she walked to school today.
c. her sister usually takes the bus, also.

The correct answer is **b**. The signal word is **but**, which signals unexpected information or contrast. It is not usual for Mary to walk to school.

Choice **a** is incorrect because it is expected information. Mary usually takes the bus, so we expect her to take it today. Choice **c** is incorrect because it is additional information (signaled by the word **also**).

1. It rained all night, so

a. it didn't rain in the morning.
b. the grass was dry in the morning.
c. the grass was wet in the morning.

2. John studied very hard for the test. However,

a. he failed the test.
b. he got a good grade on the test.
c. he passed the test.

3. The human brain has many different parts such as

a. the cerebrum, the medulla oblongata, and the cerebellum.
b. the cerebrum is located in the forebrain.
c. the thalamus and hypothalamus are two glands in the hindbrain.

4. In some cultures, certain foods are *taboo*. That is,

   a. a word in the Fiji Islands language.
   b. people are not allowed to eat certain foods.
   c. why people do not eat them.

5. The most popular pets in the United States are dogs and cats although

   a. some people prefer birds as pets.
   b. many people like dogs and cats.
   c. many people in the United States have pets.

6. Rafael's native language is Spanish. In addition,

   a. he speaks Spanish.
   b. he can speak Italian and German.
   c. he is living in Japan.

7. An ancient Hindu book says that people who commit various crimes will be born in the bodies of animals in their next lives. For example,

   a. the title of the book is *The Laws of Manu*.
   b. the elephant is a noble animal.
   c. if someone steals grain, he is reborn as a rat.

8. John could not study for the test last night, but

   a. he failed the test.
   b. he can't study today.
   c. he passed the test.

9. John could not study for the test last night because

   a. he failed the test.
   b. he was working.
   c. he passed the test.

10. The brain causes us to perform actions that require thinking, such as running or shaking hands. We do these things on purpose. The brain also

    a. causes us to do some things that do not require thinking, such as breathing.
    b. causes us to run and to shake hands.
    c. causes us to do things on purpose, such as running and shaking hands.

Adjective Clause Review

You learned about adjective clauses in Chapter 2. Adjective clauses modify nouns and noun phrases. They frequently begin with one of the following words:

people	**who, whom, that**	places	**where, in which**
things	**that, which**	time	**when**

Read each question below. Find the answers in the reading selection. Write the answers on the blank lines. Each answer should include the adjective clause and the noun or noun phrase that it modifies. The first one is done for you.

Paragraph 2

1. Which religions believe that we have one life here followed by one life after death?

   *the three religions that originated in the **Middle East***

2. Which religions believe that we have a succession of different lives?

   _____

Paragraph 3

3. Who believe that we were not human beings in all of our past lives?

   _____

Paragraph 4

4. What do Hindus and Buddhists regard as desirable to escape from?

   _____

Paragraph 5

5. In third stage (of the *Bardo*), what does the person move toward?

   _____

Paragraph 6

6. Who may be born as a rich and happy person in the next life?

_____

7. Who will pay in the next life for bad deeds?

_____

Paragraph 7

8. Who will be born in the bodies of animals in their next lives?

_____

9. Who is reborn as a rat?

_____

Paragraph 8

10. What are the heavens and hells of believers in rebirth?

_____

_____

Text Mapping: Topics and Details

Below is a list of the main topics and the details about the main topics of paragraph 2 of the reading selection.

Write each one in the correct box on page 138. Some have already been done for you. They are marked with a check (✔). Look back at paragraph 2 to help you.

✔■ today there are two principal beliefs concerning life after death

■ Judaism, Christianity, and Islam

■ Hinduism and Buddhism

■ we have one life here followed by one life after death

■ Middle East

✔■ India

■ we have a succession of different lives

✔■ this belief is called reincarnation or rebirth

■ each life is spent in a different body

■ after we die in one body, we will be born again in another body

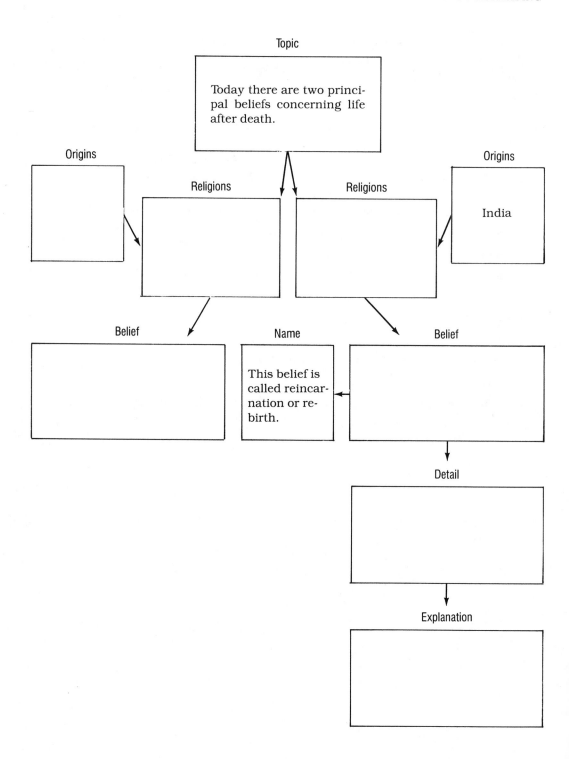

Topic

Today there are two principal beliefs concerning life
after death.

Origins

Religions

Religions

Origins

India

Belief

Name

Belief

This belief is
called reincar-
nation or re-
birth.

Detail

Explanation

Below is a list of the main topic and details of paragraph 3.

   Write each one in the correct box below. Look back at paragragh 3 of the reading selection to help you.

- many believers in rebirth believe that we were not human beings in all of our past lives
- in some we might have been gods or supernatural beings
- in some we might have been animals
- not harming animals is sometimes part of the ethics of believers in rebirth
- the souls or minds of animals might at one time have been in human bodies

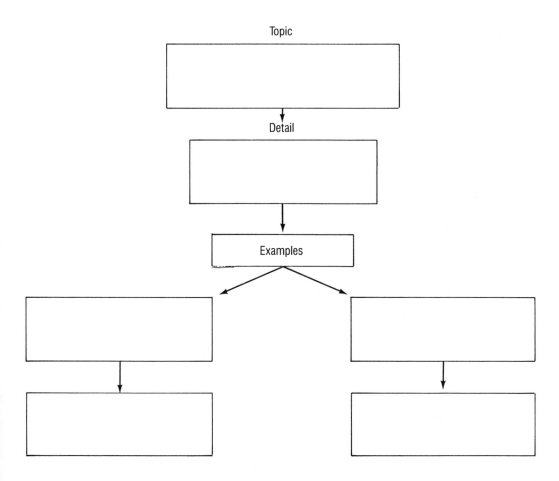

Comprehension Questions

Answer the following questions by circling **True** or **False**, by writing the answer on the blank lines, or by circling the letter of the correct answer. If a statement is false, explain why it is false.

Paragraph 1

1. **True** or **False**   Sixty thousand years ago, our distant ancestors probably thought that there was another life after the one here.

Paragraph 2

2. What are the two principal beliefs concerning a life after death?

   _____

   _____

3. What is reincarnation or rebirth?

   _____

Paragraph 3

4. In line 2, "them" refers to

   a. those who believe in rebirth.
   b. human beings.
   c. our past lives.

5. Why is not harming or eating animals sometimes part of the ethics of believers in rebirth?

   _____

Paragraph 4

6. **Line 6**   What do the words "This state" refer to?

_____

7. **True** or **False**   Hindus and Buddhists regard it as desirable to escape *sansara* and attain *nirvana*.

Paragraph 6

8. **Line 7**   The words "On the other hand" signal a contrast. What is the contrast?

   a. between good deeds and bad deeds
   b. between what will happen to someone who does good deeds and what will happen to someone who does bad deeds
   c. between rich and happy people and poor and unhappy people

Paragraph 7

9. **True** or **False**   Animals can attain *nirvana*.

Paragraph 8

10. **True** or **False**   The heavens and hells of believers in rebirth are permanent.

✎ Writing Assignment

Look back at your text map of paragraph 2 on page 138. Write a short three-or four- sentence summary of the paragraph using *only* the map. Do *not* look back at the reading selection.

   Write only what you think is important. You do not have to write everything that is on the map. Use your own sentences. Do the same with the map of paragraph 6.

For thousands of years, Chinese children have been taught to honor and respect their parents. *Courtesy of United Nations.*

8 Filial Piety or Reverence for Parents

In small groups, discuss the following:

- What is the relationship between parents and children in your culture?
- For example, what do parents expect from their children?
- Are there special things children should/must do for their parents?
- What are these things?
- Does the oldest son or daughter have special responsibilities toward the parent?
- What happens when parents get old or ill — who takes care of them?

Use your dictionary to find the meaning of the following verbs:

> **honor**
> **revere**
> **worship**

and the following noun:

> **ceremony**

READING SELECTION

Filial Piety or Reverence for Parents

There is probably no society or culture where children are not expected to show some respect for their parents. The fifth of the ten commandments followed by both Jews and Christians tells us to honor our father and our mother. In Asia, respect for parents has always been particularly important, more so than it is in the West. In China, it has been, perhaps, more important than in any other country. The Chinese have a word, *hsiao* (shee-ow), which is often translated as "filial piety." "Reverence for parents" is also a good translation. The character for *hsiao* is written

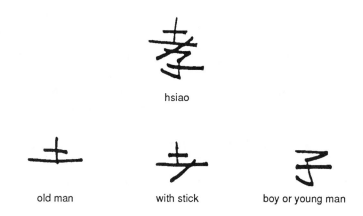

hsiao

old man   with stick   boy or young man

and is supposed to represent an old man with a stick leaning on a boy or young man.

(2)   Even before the time of Confucius, which was 2500 years ago, reverence for parents was an important part of Chinese life. Confucius was China's greatest philosopher, and he was also a great advocate of *hsiao*. Because of the influence of his support, it has been important throughout China's history. According to Confucius, the filial son (one who has reverence for his parents) should act in such a way that his parents will not have to worry about him. He should not even travel very far from his home when his parents are alive. He should take care of his body, even down to his fingernails, because it is the gift of his parents. He should act so that he has a good reputation and even try to become famous, all in order to honor his parents.

(3)   Another important value for the ancient Chinese was *li*, which means ceremony or correct behavior. Much of social life and the relations between people was governed by rules. There were rules as to how sons should behave with fathers, younger brothers with elder brothers, and friends with friends. Offerings of food and drink were made to dead ancestors and to other supernatural beings. Such offerings or sacrifices were governed by *li* as were weddings, funerals, and special holidays. Filial reverence was a part of *li*. Confucius said that when parents were alive, they should be treated according to *li*. When they died, they should be buried according to *li*. After their death, they should be sacrificed to according to *li*.

(4)   The idea of reverence for parents is closely connected to what is sometimes called "ancestor worship," although this is not an accurate term. A better term might be reverence for ancestors. Reverence for parents does not stop after they are dead. They continue to be revered as ancestors. According to *li*, offerings of food and drink ("sacrifices") should be made to them, and various ceremonies honoring them should be performed.

(5)   The Chinese believed that the well-being of the living and the dead were connected. The family group, or clan, included both the living and the dead. Deceased members of the clan were to be treated right by the living members by means of appropriate ceremonies and offerings. Then the ancestors would see to it that things went well for the living members of the clan.

(6)   Appropriate burial of ancestors was linked to their well-being. Among other things, this meant that a good place or site should be found in which to bury them. Experts on *feng-shui* (wind and water) were hired to advise families about the right site for burial. Stories are told about an ancestor's body being moved from one site to another in the hope of improving the good fortune of the family or clan.

(7)   An understanding of *hsiao* can help one to appreciate some of the incidents that occur in Chinese literature. In China's greatest classical novel, *The Dream of the Red Chamber*, there are a number of such incidents. In one, the hero of the novel, a young boy called Pao Yu, gets in trouble with his father. His father has the servants hold him and tells them: "Beat him to death." While Pao Yu is being beaten, word spreads through the family mansion of what is happening and reaches the boy's grandmother, the father's mother. The grandmother arrives at the room where her grandson is being beaten and orders her son to stop. Just as *hsiao* gives the father the right to beat his son, so it obliges him to stop when his mother tells him to.

(8)   Throughout much of its history, Japan has been greatly influenced by Chinese philosophy and literature. Many of the ways of traditional China, such as *hsiao*, were absorbed at an early date. The seventeenth-century

Japanese philosopher, Nakae Toju, says that if filial piety is torn from someone's heart, they become like a plant without roots. He goes on to say that although it would seem that an orphan has no obligations to filial piety, this is not so. To care for one's moral nature is a filial obligation whether our parents are living or dead. According to this thinking, becoming the best kind of human being we can be is the highest reverence we can give our parents.

EXERCISES

Scanning Questions

Look back at the reading selection to find the answers to the following questions.

Paragraph 1

1. What has, perhaps, been more important in China than in any other country?

_____

2. What are two ways of translating the Chinese word *hsaio*?

_____

Paragraph 2

3. According to Confucius, how should the filial son act?

_____

4. Why should the filial son take care of his body?

_____

Paragraph 3

5. What does *li* mean?

   _____

6. What was governed by rules in ancient China?

   _____

7. What are three examples in this paragraph of relations between people (that were governed by rules)?

   _____

   _____

   _____

Paragraph 4

8. What does not stop after parents are dead?

   _____

9. According to *li*, what "sacrifices" should be made to parents after they are dead?

   _____

Paragraph 5

10. What did the Chinese believe were connected?

    _____

11. How were deceased members of the clan to be treated right by the living members?

    _____

12. Then what would the ancestors do?

    _____

Paragraph 6

13. What was one thing that appropriate burial of ancestors meant?

_____

14. Who were hired to advise families about the right site for burial?

_____

15. Why was an ancestor's body moved from place to place?

_____

Paragraph 8

16. According to Nakae Toju, what happens if filial piety is torn from someone's heart?

_____

17. What is a filial obligation whether our parents are living or dead?

_____

Vocabulary

Fill in the blanks with the correct words from the list below. Sentence **a** of each pair is from the reading selection. Sentence **b** uses the same word with the same meaning as in sentence **a**.

accurate	continue(d)	represent(s)	respect
advocate(s)	govern(ed)	reputation	

1a. There is probably no society or culture where children are not expected to show some _____ for their parents.

  b. We should show _____ for the flag of our country. For example, we should not put it on the ground or step on it.

2a. The character for *hsaio* is written ![character 孝] and is supposed

to _____ an old man with a stick leaning on a boy or young man.

b. Our flag _____ our country.

3a. Confucius was China's greatest philosopher, and he was also a great

_____ of *hsaio*.

b. Some people think a good diet is most important for a person's

health. Other people are _____ of exercise as the most important thing for health.

4a. He should act so that he has a good _____ and even try to become famous.

b. Because Mary often takes care of sick people, she has the

_____ of being a kind and helpful person.

5a. Much of social life and the relations between people was

_____ by rules.

b. The movements of the balls that bump into each other on a billiard

table are _____ by the laws of physics. In each collision, the balls obey the laws of physics.

6a. The idea of reverence for parents is closely connected to what is sometimes called "ancestor worship," although this is not an

_____ term.

b. Although a donkey looks a lot like a horse, it would not be

_____ to call it a horse.

7a. They _____ to be revered as ancestors.

b. They were all happy that he agreed to _____ as president for another four years.

Do the same with the following:

absorb(ed)   incident(s)   influence(d)   oblige(s)
advise   include(d)   obligation

8a. The family group, or clan, _____ both the living and the dead.

b. The furniture in the room _____ a table and four chairs.

9a. Experts on *feng-shui* (wind and water) were hired to

_____ families about the right site for burial.

b. I don't know if I should go to college next year or not. What would

you _____ me to do?

10a. An understanding of *hsaio* can help one to appreciate some of the

_____ that occur in Chinese literature.

b. John was late for work yesterday because of a succession of unfor-

tunate _____. First, he could not find his car keys. Next, his car would not start. Then he missed the bus.

11a. Just as *hsaio* gives the father the right to beat his son, so it

_____ him to stop when his mother tells him to.

b. Being a good parent _____ me to help my children with their homework.

12a. Throughout much of its history, Japan has been greatly

_____ by Chinese philosophy and literature.

b. I had great respect for one of my teachers, so I was

_____ by his advice about my future.

13a. Many of the ways of traditional China, such as *hsaio* were

_____ at an early date.

b. She studied the chapter assigned for homework until she had

_____ most of it. Then she felt that she would pass
the test.

14a. To care for one's moral nature is a filial _____ whether
one's parents are living or dead.

b. Good parents feel an _____ to help their children with
their homework.

Self-Test

Fill in the blank lines with the correct words from the list below.

absorbed	advocate	incidents	obligation	reputation
accurate	continue	included	obliges	respect
advise	governed	influenced	represent	

1. A ball that is thrown upwards is _____ by the law of
   gravity, so eventually it will come down.

2. My watch always has the correct time. It is very _____.

3. He is a strong _____ of recycling. He thinks it is very
   important for the world.

4. I play baseball a lot, and I have the _____ of being a
   very good player.

5. He was older than I was, and I admired him, so I treated him with

   great _____.

6. The child drew a picture with four legs, a body, and a head. It was

   supposed to _____ a dog.

7. John thought that Mary was acting strangely. There had been sev-

   eral _____ that made him worry about her.

8. I enjoy walking, and I intend to _____ doing it as long
   as I can.

9. I _____ you not to do that. I think that it is dangerous.

10. He _____ everything the teacher said and repeated it
    afterward.

11. His opinion of people is _____ by the kind of clothes
    that they wear and the kind of car they drive.

12. John and Mary were _____ among the people who
    were invited to the party.

13. Being a good person _____ one to help others.

14. Because Rex was his dog, he felt an _____ to take care
    of him.

Words with More Than One Meaning

Study each set of sentences below. Sentence **a** of each set is from the vocabulary exercises you have already studied. Sentence **b** and sentence **c** of each set use the same word with two different meanings.

Below each set are three meanings. Write the letter of the appropriate sentence in front of each meaning. The first one has been done for you.

1a. Do you like only **certain** kinds of books, like mysteries, or do you like a lot of different kinds of stories?

b. Are you **certain** that it will rain tomorrow?
Yes. The weatherman says there is a 95% chance of rain tomorrow.

c. You should save a **certain** amount of money each month.

- _**b**_ sure
- _**c**_ a specific amount
- _**a**_ a few out of many

2a. She **committed** an error when she trusted him. He stole some money from her.

b. He is very **committed** to his job. He works 70 hours a week.

c. The President has not **committed** himself about higher taxes.

- _____ said what he is going to do
- _____ make, do
- _____ feels very strongly about

3a. Students don't like to sit in the front of a classroom. They usually **concentrate** in the seats in the back of the room.

b. I don't like to play music while I am doing my homework. I can't **concentrate** on my homework when the music is playing.

c. The power of the government is **concentrated** in the president.

- _____ gather together in one area
- _____ put one's attention on something
- _____ centered

4a. The president of a company is **involved** with the overall management of the company.
  b. A word processor is much more **involved** than a typewriter.
  c. Mary is very **involved** in the International Students Club. She attends all the meetings and goes to most of the activities.

_____ complex, complicated
_____ takes an active part in
_____ is connected to

5a. Some people **regard** rock music as great music. Other people think rock music is bad.
  b. It gave me great joy when I **regarded** my baby's face for the first time.
  c. Professor Smith is an excellent teacher. I have great **regard** for him.

_____ have an opinion about something
_____ think very highly of someone
_____ look at

6a. Smoking is **responsible** for many deaths from lung cancer.
  b. John is a very **responsible** person. You can depend on him to do his job.
  c. Mary said that she would be **responsible** for bringing the food to the picnic.

_____ source, cause
_____ agree to do something that is needed
_____ reliable

7a. When John asked Mary to marry him, she **treated** him very badly. She laughed and told him to go away.
  b. The doctor **treated** the injured man.
  c. At the end of the class, the teacher **treated** the students to ice cream.

_____ pay for
_____ behave toward
_____ give medical aid

8a. In my **view**, it is very important to eat a healthy diet. Other people think that exercise is the most important.

  b. The **view** from the top of the hill is beautiful. You can see the lake and the mountains.

  c. He is studying Biology, Chemistry, and Physics with a **view** to becoming a medical student.

    _____ opinion, belief
    _____ scenery
    _____ purpose, intention

9a. A two-liter bottle can contain a greater **volume** of liquid than a one-liter bottle can.

  b. A good library has many **volumes**.

  c. That music is too loud. Please lower the **volume**.

    _____ books
    _____ loudness of sound
    _____ amount of space to hold something

Synonyms

Below are seven sentences with one word underlined in each sentence. Below each sentence are three more words. One of these three words is a synonym of the underlined word in that sentence. Draw a circle around the word that is a synonym for the underlined word.

▥➡ *Example*

    Every year on my birthday, he gives me a nice gift.

    (reward, present, message)

  1. I am certain that it is going to rain tomorrow.

    (sure, conscious, doubtful)

  2. It is not liable to rain tomorrow.

    (certain, likely, predictable)

3. For this job, we need someone who is very <u>responsible</u>.

   (reliable, involved, determined)

4. Many critics <u>regard</u> Emily Dickinson as one of the greatest women poets.

   (situation, conscious, view)

5. The idea of a Christmas tree <u>originated</u> in Germany.

   (centered, began, failed)

6. In the American Southwest, it gets extremely hot in the summer. It is not a good <u>area</u> to visit in the summer.

   (direction, opportunity, region)

7. A shovel is not a very <u>complex</u> tool.

   (complicated, ordinary, creative)

Antonyms

Below is a list of words followed by eight sentences. There is one underlined word in each sentence. The list of words contains **antonyms** for the underlined words. An antonym is a word that is opposite in meaning to another word. For example, the words *happy* and *unhappy* are antonyms.

Decide which word from the list is an antonym for each underlined word and rewrite each sentence using the antonym. Be sure that the sentence makes sense.

⫸ *Example*

> Mary was very <u>happy</u> with her job, so she enjoyed going to work every day.

Rewritten: Mary was very <u>unhappy</u> with her job, so she didn't enjoy going to work every day.

(It would not make sense to say that Mary was very unhappy with her job, so she *enjoyed* going to work every day.)

abnormal	disappear	temporary	unconscious
complete	stop	uncomplicated	unfavorable

1. If the weather is <u>favorable</u> tomorrow, we will go to the beach.

_____

_____

2. When it gets dark, stars <u>appear</u> in the sky.

_____

_____

3. My job is <u>permanent</u>, so I will not have to find another job soon.

_____

_____

4. It is <u>normal</u> for a dog to walk on four feet.

_____

_____

5. If it <u>continues</u> snowing, we will be able to go skiing tomorrow.

_____

_____

6. After the accident, the man was <u>conscious</u> and could talk.

_____

_____

7. My packing is <u>incomplete</u>, and I am not ready to go.

_____

_____

8. A computer is very <u>complex</u> compared to a hand calculator.

_____

_____

Comprehension Questions

Answer the following questions by filling in the blank lines or by circling the correct answer. If a statement is false, explain why it is false.

Paragraph 1

1. **True** or **False**   Jews and Christians are expected to show respect for their parents.

2. In line 6, "it" refers to _____

Paragraph 2

3. **True** or **False**   Reverence for parents has been important in China throughout history because Confucius supported it.

4. What is a filial son? _____

5. Which of the following should a filial son do in order to honor his parents? Circle all the correct answers.

   a. not cause his parents to worry about him
   b. take care of his body
   c. travel around the world
   d. act so he has a good reputation
   e. live quietly so that not many people know him

Paragraph 3

6. **True** or **False**   The rules of *li* were only for living people.

Paragraph 4

7. What should the living do to show reverence for their dead parents?

_____

_____

Paragraph 5

8. Which one of the following is true?

   a. The ancient Chinese did not believe that the deceased members of the clan could help the living members, so they did not make offerings to them.
   b. The ancient Chinese had ceremonies and made offerings to the deceased members of the clan because they believed these things would help the dead in another world.
   c. The ancient Chinese had ceremonies and made offerings to the deceased members of the clan because they believed the dead could help the living in this world.

Paragraph 6

9. **True** or **False**   The ancient Chinese believed that burying an ancestor in the right place would help the living.

Paragraph 7

10. **True** or **False**   The father stopped beating his son because of filial piety.

Paragraph 8

11. **True** or **False**   The obligations of filial piety stop when both parents are dead.

✍ Writing Assignment

- Do children have special obligations toward parents?
- Do parents have special obligations toward their children?
- Who takes care of the parents when they are old?

Write about the relationship between parents and children in your culture.

A: Feather representing *ma'at*
B: The heart of a person who has just died

Osiris, the Egyptian god and judge of the dead, determines the final judgment: eternal life or eternal death. *From the papyrus of Ani, No. 10470, Sheets 3 and 4. Courtesy of the British Museum.*

<table>
<tr><td>

9

</td><td>

Law and Order

</td></tr>
</table>

In small groups, discuss the following.

- What is your daily routine?

  When do you usually get up?
  Do you eat breakfast first or do you get dressed first?
  What times during the day do you eat?
  When do you usually go to work or to school?

- Do you like to have routine in your life?
- Do you like to clean your house in a certain order?
- Do you brush your teeth a certain way?
- Do you have a routine for doing your homework?
- Should ceremonies — such as weddings, funerals, and graduations — be performed in a certain way? How should they be performed?
- What kind of social rules do you follow — such as shaking hands when you meet someone or visiting someone's house? (Do you take off your hat or your shoes when you visit someone?)
- What would happen to society if there were no laws?
- Would there be any police if there weren't any laws?
- How is order demonstrated in the universe — such as the sun rising and the movements (orbits) of the planets around the sun?
- What happens when you throw something up in the air?
- What is the "law" that makes the object fall back to the ground?
- What would happen if the universe were not ordered — that is, if the planets did not move according to a pattern?

161

READING SELECTION

Law and Order

All modern scientists believe that there is an order to the universe. That is, that physical things obey certain laws. If I hit a ball in a certain way, for example, then it will start to move in a certain direction with a certain speed. We say that the ball obeys the laws of motion. Although an ordered universe is necessary for scientific thinking, the idea of an ordered universe is much older than science.

(2)   The ancient Sumerians, who lived in what is today called Iraq, did not believe in an ordered universe. They believed the universe was ruled by gods, who did whatever they wanted to do without any reason. The Sumerians probably believed this because unpredictable natural changes occurred in their land, such as floods, that they could not control. Perhaps because they found the universe unpredictable, they tried to make up for it in their society. They had a strong sense of order and justice in the affairs of men, which they called *me*. The Sumerians and their successors, the Babylonians, had sets of laws to deal with many different situations. The name of one of the Babylonian lawgivers, Hammurabi, is famous to this day.

(3)   Unlike the Sumerians, the ancient Egyptians had a strong feeling that the universe was ordered. This was probably due to the regularity with which the Nile River flooded every year, bringing water to the fields and crops. The sun also was extremely important to them, and it was even more regular in its movements than the Nile. The Egyptians also believed in an orderly society, in which people acted as they were expected to. They viewed an orderly society as an extension of the order in the universe. They called this orderliness in the universe *ma'at*. At the end of any ceremony involving their gods, they held up a little statue of *ma'at* facing the statue of the god.

(4)   The Egyptians believed in a last judgment when they died, which decided whether they would die forever or live forever in a sort of hereafter. In this judgment, the god Osiris, judge of the dead, weighed the heart of the person who had just died against a feather representing *ma'at*. The heart had to weigh exactly what the feather did in order for the person to live forever.

(5)   The ancient people of India also believed in an order to the universe, which they called *rita. Rita* was protected by the god Varuna. *Rita* referred both to natural order and to order in society. Order in society was

preserved by *dharma*, or duty. Everyone was supposed to follow *dharma*, that is, to do whatever was their duty. The Indians had an elaborate system of caste, in which your birth determined the occupation you could follow and your relationship to other people. The highest caste was that of the priests. A person's duty depended on which caste he or she belonged to.

(6)   The great Indian epic called the *Mahabharata* has an interesting story about *dharma*. One of the heroes in the epic has followed a long difficult path towards heaven and is finally very near. His faithful dog has accompanied him on his entire journey, after everyone else has dropped by the wayside. A supernatural being appears to the hero of the story and tells him that he can go to heaven but that his dog cannot. The hero refuses to abandon his dog, even if it means he will not go to heaven. The dog then reveals himself to be the god *Dharma*. By not abandoning his duty to his dog, the hero has passed the last test and is able to go to heaven.

(7)   In ancient times, there were two great philosophies in China. One, Confucianism, was founded by a real historical person called Confucius. The other, Taoism, was believed to have been founded by a probably mythical figure called Lao Tzu, a name that means "old master." Both these philosophies believed in an order to the universe, which they called the *tao*, usually translated as "the way." For the Confucians, the *tao* was something created by people, the order of society. For the Taoists, the *tao* was something that was impossible to describe, but that was at the heart of the universe.

(8)   The *Taoist Way* is not easy to understand. The opening lines of the book supposedly written by Lao Tzu say that the Way that can be spoken of is not the real Way. Lao Tzu and the other Taoists love mystery, and they also love sayings that seem to contradict themselves. One of his sayings is that to be crooked is to become straight and that to be empty is to become full.

(9)   Confucius believed in an ordered universe, and he believed in an ordered society as well. Much of the order in Chinese society was achieved by people following the rules of conduct, which were called *li*. *Li* gave people rules for what was right and wrong, but it went beyond dealing with right and wrong since many of the details of everyday living had to be done in particular ways in order to follow *li*.

(10)   Although the people of Europe did not have anything that was the equivalent of *ma'at, rita,* or *tao,* they too believed in an ordered universe. Both Christians and Jews believed in one God, a God whose laws were to be obeyed by the sun and stars as well as by men. Many people think that this belief in divine law led to a belief in natural law and that this was the reason that modern science originated in Europe.

EXERCISES

Scanning Questions

Look back at the Reading Selection to find the answers to the following questions.

Paragraph 1

1. What do all modern scientists believe?

_____

2. What is necessary for scientific thinking?

_____

Paragraph 2

3. Did the ancient Sumerians believe in an ordered universe?

_____

4. Who did the Sumerians think the universe was ruled by?

_____

Paragraph 3

5. Did the ancient Egyptians believe that the universe was ordered?

_____

6. How did the ancient Egyptians view an orderly society?

_____

7. What did the ancient Egyptians call orderliness in the universe?

_____

Paragraph 5

8. Did the ancient people of India believe in an order to the universe?

_____

9. How was order in society preserved in ancient India?

_____

10. What did a person's duty depend on?

_____

Paragraph 6

11. How did the hero pass the last test?

_____

Paragraph 7

12. What were the names of the two philosophies in ancient China?

_____

13. Who founded each one?

_____

14. Did both of these philosophies believe in an order to the universe?

_____

15. What did they call this order to the universe?

_____

Paragraph 8

16. What do Lao Tzu and the other Taoists love?

_____

17. What is an example of a saying that seems to contradict itself?

_____

Paragraph 10

18. Did the people of Europe believe in an ordered universe?

_____

19. What do many people think that this European belief in divine law led to?

_____

Vocabulary

Fill in the blank lines with the correct words from the list below. Sentence **a** of each pair is from the reading selection. Sentence **b** uses the same word as sentence **a** with the same meaning.

duty	obey(s)	regular	weigh(ed)
extension	order	(un)predictable	

1a. All modern scientists believe that there is an _____ to the universe.

b. We say that there is _____ in something if its parts form a pattern and we can know what it will do.

2a. We say that the ball _____ the laws of motion.

  b. Bill watches road signs when he drives, and he does what the signs

  tell him to. He _____ the traffic laws.

3a. The Sumerians probably believed this because _____
natural changes occurred in their land, such as floods, that they
could not control.

  b. He is completely _____. I never know what he is going
to do next.

4a. The sun also was extremely important to them, and it was even

  more _____ in its movements than the Nile.

  b. A watch that is not _____ in its movements does not
keep accurate time.

5a. They viewed an orderly society as an _____ of the
order in the universe.

  b. Getting a job in a bookstore was an _____ of her liking
for books.

6a. In this judgment, the god Osiris, judge of the dead,

  _____ the heart of the person who had just died
against a feather representing *ma'at*.

  b. The cashier _____ the tomatoes I was buying. They

  _____ three pounds.

7a. Order in society was preserved by *dharma*, or _____.

  b. In some societies, it is the _____ of the oldest son to
take care of his parents when they are old.

Do the same with the following:

achieve(d)   determine(s), (ed)   equivalent
contradict(s)   elaborate   mythical

8a. The Indians had an _____ system of caste, in which your birth determined the occupation you could follow and your relationship to other people.

b. The king's uniform was very _____. It had many gold buttons and decorations of gold and silver on it.

9a. The Indians had an elaborate system of caste, in which your birth

_____ the occupation you could follow and your relationship to other people.

b. Your age _____ whether or not you can buy alcoholic drinks at a restaurant. You must be twenty-one years old in order to buy alcohol.

10a. The other, Taoism, was believed to have been founded by a probably

_____ figure called Lao Tzu, a name that means "old master."

b. A myth is a story made up about gods or heroes, and a

_____ person is one who never existed although he appears in these stories.

11a. Lao Tzu and the other Taoists love mystery and they also love say-

ings that seem to _____ themselves.

b. She always _____ anything that I say. No matter what I say, she disagrees with it.

12a. Much of the order in Chinese society was _____ by people following the rules of conduct, which were called *li*.

b. Good grades in school are _____ by hard work and study.

13a. Although the people of Europe did not have anything that was the

_____ of *ma'at, rita,* or *tao,* they too believed in an

ordered universe.

b. Many people feel that when a drunk driver kills someone in an acci-

dent, it is _____ to murder.

Self-Test

Fill in the blank lines with the correct words from the list below.

achieved	duty	extension	order	weighs
contradicts	elaborate	mythical	regular	
determined	equivalent	obey	unpredictable	

1. I have a small dog. He _____ only ten pounds.

2. It is the _____ of a policeman to try to prevent crime.

3. All good citizens should _____ the law.

4. Chess pieces are arranged in a particular _____ on the
   chessboard at the beginning of a game.

5. His enjoyment of jazz is an _____ of his love for music.

6. In my country, tornados can appear without warning. They are very

   _____.

7. The guards marched past the gate every ten minutes. They were

   very _____ in their movements.

8. I ran around the block eight times, which was the

   _____ of running three miles.

9. It was a very _____ rug. The pattern was very compli-cated with many different colors.

10. The weather report on one TV channel says that it is going to rain tomorrow. However, another channel _____ that. According to the other channel, it is going to be a sunny day tomorrow.

11. The salary that a teacher receives is _____ by the number of years she or he has taught.

12. When I was a little child, I believed in Santa Claus. Now I know he is a _____ being.

13. Many people think that happiness can be _____ only by making other people happy.

Signal Words

If   **If** signals a condition. The clause that begins with **if** is the condition. The second clause in the sentence is the result.
          The condition must happen or be true in order for the result to happen or be true.

Condition	Result of the Condition Happening or Being True
If it rains tomorrow	we will not have a picnic.

What will the result be if it rains tomorrow?
We will not have a picnic.

Read the sentences below and answer the questions.

1. Baby birds will instinctively run away if the cardboard shape of a hawk is moved forwards over their heads.

   What is the condition?

   _____

   What is the result of the condition happening?

   _____

2. However, they do not run if the cardboard shape is moved backwards.

   What is the result of the cardboard shape being moved backwards?

   _____

3. If our right hand is injured, we can learn to write with our left.

   Under what condition can we learn to write with our left hand?

   _____

4. If a man steals honey, he is reborn as a bee.

   What causes a man to be reborn as a bee?

   _____

5. The seventeenth-century Japanese philosopher, Nakae Toju, says that if filial piety is torn from someone's heart, he becomes like a plant without roots.

   What is the condition?

   _____

   What is the result of the condition being true?

   _____

Signal Word Review

Answer the following questions:

Paragraph 1

1. There are two words that signal an explanation. What are they?

   _____

   What is being explained?

   _____

   What is the explanation?

   _____

2. What word in this paragraph signals a condition?

   _____

   What is the condition?

   _____

   What is the result of the condition happening?

   _____

3. The words "for example" signal that the condition is an example of something. What is it an example of?

   _____

Paragraph 2

4. What is the first word in this paragraph that signals a cause?

_____

What is the cause?

_____

What is the result?

_____

5. What two words in this paragraph signal an example?

_____

What is the example?

_____

What is it an example of?

_____

6. Result: they tried to make up for it in their society

Cause: _____

Paragraph 5

7. What is the explanation for "to follow *dharma*"?

_____

Paragraph 9

8. In the first sentence, the words "as well" signal additional information. What two things did Confucius believe in?

_____

9. In the third sentence, the word "since" means "because." That is, in this sentence "since" signals a cause. Why does *li* go beyond dealing with right and wrong?

_____

Word Families

Listed below are different forms of some of the vocabulary words in Chapters 7, 8, and 9. The new forms are different parts of speech. Study them before you do the exercise.

Verbs	*Nouns*	*Adjectives*	*Adverbs*
accumulate	accumulation	accumulated	——
——	accuracy	accurate/ inaccurate	accurately
harm	harm	harmful	harmfully
influence	influence	influential	——
originate	origin	——	——
predict	prediction	predictable/ unpredictable	predictably
——	regularity	regular/irregular	regularly
respect	respect	respectful/ disrespectful	respectfully

Adjective Ending

-ful   which means **full of**
harmful   full of harm
respectful full of respect

Fill in the blanks with the correct word.

1. accumulate   accumulation   accumulated

   a. When I woke up this morning, there was an _____
      of ten inches of snow on the ground. The snow

      _____ was difficult to shovel.

   b. Some people love books, and they buy them often. Over a long

      period of time, these people _____ large private
      libraries of their own.

2. accuracy   accurate/inaccurate   accurately

   a. Miss Jones is a very _____ typist. She makes very
      few mistakes. Mr. Smith makes many mistakes. He is an

      _____ typist.

   b. The _____ of your typing is very important for this
      job. You probably won't get the job if you can't type.

3. harmed   harm   harmful

   a. Cigarette smoking is _____ to your health.

   b. The temperature went below freezing one night in May. The freez-

      ing temperature _____ many of the spring flowers
      in my garden.

   c. That dog is very gentle. He won't cause you any

      _____ if you play with him.

4. influenced   influence   influential

   a. One of my teachers was very _____ in my life. His

     advice _____ my career choice. Because of his

     _____, I am now working in a job that I like.

5. originated   origins

   a. Some people believe that the _____ of all human
     beings were in Africa. That is, they believe that the ancestors of

     all modern humans _____ in Africa.

6. predict   predictions   predictable/unpredictable

   a. Modern computers make weather _____ more ac-

     curate. Weathermen can now _____ the weather
     more accurately.

   b. John's weekday schedule is very _____. He always
     gets up at the same time, goes to work at the same time, and
     comes home at the same time. However, on weekends, his sched-

     ule is _____. Sometimes he sleeps late, and some-
     times he gets up early. Some weekends he plays tennis in the
     morning. Other weekends he plays tennis in the afternoon.

7. regularity   regular/irregular   regularly

   a. Our current mailman is very _____. He always de-
     livers the mail around 10:30. The previous mailman was very

     _____. We never knew what time he would deliver

     the mail. We are happy with the _____ of our mail
     delivery now.

   b. John exercises _____. He does some form of exer-
     cise every day.

8. respected   disrespectful   respectfully

    a. Children should speak _____ to their parents.

    b. Because I _____ my uncle, I always listened to his advice.

    c. It is _____ to step on the flag of your country.

Comprehension Questions

Read each of the following statements and circle **True** or **False**. If the statement is false, explain why it is false.

Paragraph 1
1. **True** or **False**   A ball obeying the laws of motion is an example of order in the universe.

Paragraph 2
2. **True** or **False**   The Sumerians possibly developed an ordered society because the natural changes in their land were not predictable (ordered).

Paragraph 3
3. **True** or **False**   The flooding of the Nile River in Egypt was not predictable.

4. **True** or **False**   The predictable movements of the sun was probably one reason why the Egyptians believed that the universe was ordered.

5. **True** or **False**   In an orderly society, people do whatever they want to do.

Paragraph 5

   6. **True** or **False**   In ancient India, order in society was achieved by everyone doing his or her duty.

   7. **True** or **False**   Everyone's duty was the same.

Paragraph 7

   8. **True** or **False**   Lao Tzu was a famous historical person.

   9. **True** or **False**   Confucians and Taoists did not have the same ideas about "the way."

Paragraph 10

10. **True** or **False**   The Christians and Jews of Europe believed that their god was responsible for the order of the universe.

✍ Writing Assignment: Summary

Write a summary of paragraphs 2, 3, 5, and 7 of the reading selection. Use the five steps for writing a summary that you used in Chapters 2 and 4.

Remember: Your summary should be shorter than the original paragraph. For example, for paragraph 2, you should include the main topic (belief in an ordered or unordered universe) and two or possibly three details from the paragraph.

Reprinted with special permission of King Features Syndicate, Inc. ©1990.

10 The Spear at the Edge of the Universe

In small groups, discuss the following:

- Look at the cartoon on the opposite page.
- What two things does it say about the universe?
- Do you agree with either one? Why or why not?
- How have people been able to find things out about the universe?
- What is a galaxy?
- What is the name of our galaxy?
- How do we measure the distance to the stars?
- Do you know which star is closest to the earth?
- What else do you know about the universe?

READING SELECTION

The Spear at the Edge of the Universe

More than two thousand years ago, a Greek philosopher asked a question. Suppose, he said, there is a man with a spear at the edge of the universe. What happens to his spear when he throws it? Does it bounce back? Disappear? Keep going? Obviously, the philosopher assumed that there was an edge to the universe, but perhaps he was wrong. Perhaps there is no edge to the universe.

(2)   Whether there is an edge to the universe or not, many people have spent much of their lives looking for it in different ways. Some, like the Greek philosopher, have thought about it. Others have traveled across the world in search of it. Some have only dreamed about it. For the last three hundred years, people have looked for it through larger and larger telescopes.

(3)   Originally the universe seemed to be a flat circle of earth covered by a bowl-shaped sky. However, as people traveled more, they learned more and thought more about what they learned. In this way their ideas became more complicated. One thing they studied very early was the stars. They saw that most of the stars moved all together, as if they were all painted on a revolving globe, but a few stars moved differently from the others. These stars seemed to wander around among the others, so the Greeks called them *planets* or "wanderers." In addition to the planets, they saw that the sun and the moon also wandered in relation to the stars.

(4)   Aristotle, another famous Greek philosopher, developed a picture of the universe in which the earth was at the center of everything. According to Aristotle, the sun, the moon, the planets, and the stars all revolved around the earth. Later on, a man called Ptolemy, who lived about 150 A. D., worked out in great detail the cyclic pathways or *orbits* of the planets. However, there was one Greek, a man called Aristarchus, who believed that the earth and the planets all revolved around the sun. Although he was right, he could not give any very good reasons why he was right, so no one paid much attention to him.

(5)   The outer limit of Aristotle's universe was the sphere or globe holding the fixed stars. (Perhaps the spear would bounce back from this sphere?) Another group of philosophers — the Stoics — believed that beyond the spheres of the planets, the stars were spread out over a great distance and

that finally there was only the darkness of empty space. The Stoics saw no edge to the universe.

(6)   The Aristotelian or Ptolemaic view of the universe was popular in Europe for many hundreds of years. However, in the sixteenth century there lived three men who, each in their own way, changed this thinking. Nicolaus Copernicus (1473–1543) was a Polish scientist. He spent many years developing a system of the universe, which he published in the year he died. In this system, the earth and the planets revolved about the sun. Like Ptolemy, Copernicus worked out the details of orbital motion, but his worked better than Ptolemy's.

(7)   Giordano Bruno (1548–1600) was a thinker rather than a calculator or observer. He believed that space extended infinitely far in all directions, that there were worlds (or earths) like our own scattered through it, and that living beings could be found on some of these worlds. These ideas were not in agreement with those of the Roman Catholic Church of his time and he was regarded as a heretic, that is, a person whose beliefs were contrary to the teaching of the Church. He was burned alive at the stake as a heretic.

(8)   Galileo (1564–1642) was an Italian scientist. Although he did not invent the telescope, he was the first person to use it to look at the night sky. The stars were still little points of light when seen through a telescope, but the planets were little globes or circles. It seemed to him from this that the planets were much nearer than the stars. Galileo saw that one of the planets, Jupiter, was surrounded by four smaller bodies that orbited around it. This suggested to people that Jupiter might be like the earth, only with four moons instead of one. In the night sky, there was what looked like a river of mist through the stars, which was called the Milky Way. When Galileo turned his telescope on the Milky Way, he discovered that it was not a mist but that, instead, it consisted of thousands of stars.

(9)   In the years following Galileo, people continued to look through telescopes. Using a powerful telescope, William Herschel (1738–1822) discovered a new planet that he called Uranus. He looked closely at the Milky Way and decided it was a huge group of stars in the rough shape of a disc. Our sun is one of the stars in this group. Herschel also looked at and catalogued some misty or cloudy objects called *nebulae*. Like the philosopher Kant a few years earlier, Herschel suggested that some of these nebulae might be star systems or galaxies like our own Milky Way.

(10)   Today we know that our galaxy, the Milky Way, is just one of a vast number of star systems or galaxies that are scattered through space. These galaxies can have a number of different shapes. Some are ellipses, and some are irregular blobs. The Milky Way is a spiral galaxy. It has a dense center from which spiral arms radiate out. Our sun is located rather

far out in one of the spiral arms. It is one of one hundred million stars located in our galaxy.

(11) The distances between stars and galaxies is so large that a different measurement of distance is used for them, the light year. A light year is the distance that light, traveling at 186,000 miles per second, travels in one year. Our galaxy is one hundred thousand light years in diameter. In other words, if we could travel at the speed of light, it would take us 100,000 years to go from one side of our galaxy to the other. The nearest star to us (Alpha Centauri) is a little over four light years away. The nearest big galaxy like ours, the Andromeda galaxy, is a million light years away.

EXERCISES

Scanning Questions

Look back at the reading selection to find the answers to the following questions:

Paragraph 2

1. What have many people spent much of their lives looking for in different ways?

_____

2. For the last three hundred years, what have people looked for through larger and larger telescopes?

_____

Paragraph 3

3. What did the Greeks call the stars that seemed to wander around among the others?

_____

4. In addition to the planets, what also wandered in relation to the stars?

_____

Paragraph 4

5. According to Aristotle, what revolved around the earth?

_____

6. What did Aristarchus believe?

_____

Paragraph 5

7. Did the Stoics believe that there was an edge to the universe?

_____

Paragraph 6

8. In Copernicus' system of the universe, what revolved about what?

_____

Paragraph 7

9. What did Giordano Bruno believe?

_____

_____

_____

10. What is a heretic?

_____

11. What happened to Giordano Bruno, as a heretic?

_____

Paragraph 8

12. When seen through a telescope, what did the planets look like?

_____

13. What did Galileo discover that the Milky Way consisted of?

_____

Paragraph 9

14. What new planet did William Herschel discover?

_____

15. What did Herschel decide about the Milky Way?

_____

Paragraph 10

16. What is the shape of the Milky Way galaxy?

_____

17. Where is our sun located in the Milky Way?

_____

Paragraph 11

18. What is a light year?

_____

19. What is the diameter of the Milky Way?

_____

Vocabulary

Fill in the blanks with the correct words from the list below. Sentence **a** of each pair is from the reading selection. Sentence **b** of each pair uses the same word as sentence **a** with the same meaning.

attention	details	extend(ed)	scattered
detail	disappear(ed)	observer	

1a. Does it bounce back? _____?

  b. I watched the ship as it sailed away. It got smaller and smaller until

     finally it _____, and I could not see it any more.

2a. Later on, a man called Ptolemy, who lived about 150 A.D., worked

     out in great _____ the cyclic pathways or *orbits* of the planets.

  b. If you are going to build your own house, you will need more than just a general idea of what to do. You need to know in great

     _____ all the things you have to do and how to do them.

3a. Although he was right, he could not give any very good reasons

     why he was right, so no one paid much _____ to him.

  b. My dog barked until I went over and petted him. He wasn't angry.

     He just wanted some _____.

4a. Like Ptolemy, Copernicus worked out the _____ of orbital motion, but his worked better than Ptolemy's.

  b. Moving to a new city involves many _____. You have to sell your old house, find a house in the new city, arrange to have your furniture moved, and so forth.

5a. Giordano Bruno (1548–1600) was a thinker rather than a calculator

or _____ .

  b. He liked to watch soccer games, but he did not want to play. He was

happy just to be an _____ .

6a. He believed that space _____ infinitely far in all directions, that there were worlds (or earths) like our own scattered
through it, and that living beings could be found on some of these
worlds.

  b. The fence between the two houses _____ from the
sidewalk in front all the way back to the alley.

7a. He believed that space extended infinitely far in all directions, that

there were worlds (or earths) like our own _____
through it, and that living beings could be found on these worlds.

  b. In this circle, the black dots are all concentrated together on

one side of the circle. In this circle, the black dots are

_____ throughout the circle.

Do the same with the following:

contrary	instead	surround(ed)
dense	invent	vast

8a. These ideas were not in agreement with those of the Roman Catholic Church of his time, and he was regarded as a heretic, that is, a

person whose beliefs were _____ to the teaching of
the Church.

  b. If you believe that two plus two makes three or five, your belief is

_____ to those of all mathematicians!

9a. Although he did not _____ the telescope, he was the first person to use it to look at the night sky.

b. He wanted to _____ a new flavor of ice cream, one that no one had ever produced before.

10a. Galileo saw that one of the planets, Jupiter, was

_____ by four smaller bodies that orbited around it.

b. An island is a piece of land that is _____ by water.

11a. This suggested to people that Jupiter might be like the earth, only

with four moons _____ of one.

b. I was going to play basketball tonight, but I'm tired. I think I will

stay home and watch TV _____.

12a. Today we know that our galaxy, the Milky Way, is just one of a

_____ number of star systems and galaxies that are
scattered through space.

b. The Pacific Ocean is a _____ ocean. It occupies a lot of
space.

13a. It has a _____ center from which spiral arms radiate
out.

b. The population is quite _____ in large cities. In the
country, there are fewer people in one area.

Self-Test

Fill in the blanks with the correct words from the list below.

attention	detail	extend	observer	vast
contrary	details	instead	scattered	
dense	disappear	invent	surrounded	

1. He told me how to get to his home, but there were so many

   _____ that I could not remember them all.

2. When I talk, I like to feel that people are paying _____
   to me.

3. He walked around the corner so quickly that he seemed to just

   _____.

4. The painting of the woman was in great _____. It even
   showed the freckles on her nose.

5. A good scientific _____ often knows just what to look
   for.

6. He tried to _____ his arm upwards until his hand
   touched the ceiling, but he was not tall enough.

7. He was a messy eater. He _____ food all over the floor.

8. It was a _____ forest. The trees grew very close
   together.

9. Antarctica has _____ areas where there is nothing but
   ice and snow.

10. He was always working with machinery. He hoped that some day he

    would _____ something useful.

11. An optimist believes that life is good. A pessimist believes the

    _____, that life is bad.

12. He loved to read. When I visited him one day, he was sitting on his

    sofa _____ by books. There were books on the sofa,
    books on the table beside him, and books on the floor!

13. I know that I don't want to go to college this summer, but I'm not sure

    what I want to do _____.

Organization

Most of the Reading Selection in this chapter is organized chronologically.
That is, it is organized by time.

It begins with the earliest time — about 2,000 years ago — and moves
forward to the present time.

Below are the names mentioned in the reading and some details about their beliefs and
discoveries. They are not in the correct order. Look back at the reading and write the names
and details in the correct order in the boxes on the next page. Two have been done for you.

Names	*Details*
■ William Herschel ■ Aristotle ■ Nicolaus Copernicus ■ Galileo ■ Aristarchus ■ Giordano Bruno	■ discovered the planet Uranus, catalogued nebulae ■ believed the sun, the moon, the planets, and the stars revolved around the earth ■ first person to look at the night sky with a telescope, discovered that the Milky Way consisted of stars ■ believed the earth and the planets revolved around the sun ■ believed space was infinite, was burned as a heretic ■ developed a system of the universe in which the earth and planets revolved about the sun, worked out details of orbital motion that were better than Ptolemy's

	Name	Details
1738 to 1822		
1473 to 1650		
		believed space was infinite, was burned as a heretic
2,000 years ago		
	Aristotle	

Ellipsis: Review

In Chapter 5, there was an exercise on ellipsis. Ellipsis means that sometimes words and phrases are not replaced by pronouns; they are just omitted.

⟫ *Example*

    a. Can you swim?
    b. Yes, I can.

The word *swim* is omitted in sentence **b**.

Read the following sentences and on the blank lines, write the word or words that are omitted:

   1. Mary is not the tallest child in her family, but she is the oldest.

2. Some people like hot weather, but I don't.

_____

3. There are many different kinds of lettuce. Bibb, romaine, and leaf are a few.

_____

4. One word-processing program is WordPerfect. Another is Microsoft Word.

_____

5. Some of my friends have cars. Some don't. (There are two examples of ellipsis here.)

_____

Read the sentences below and answer the questions.

1. In some of our previous lives, we might have been gods or supernatural beings. In some, we might have been animals.

When might we have been animals?

_____

2. There are three stages in the Bardo. In the first, the person is aware of a clear pure light.

In what stage of the Bardo is the person aware of a clear pure light?

_____

3. A supernatural being appears to the hero of the story and tells him that he can go to heaven but that his dog cannot.

What cannot the dog do?

_____

4. Whether there is an edge to the universe or not, many people have spent much of their lives looking for it in different ways. Some have only dreamed about it. Others have traveled across the world in search of it.

Who have only dreamed about it?

_____

Who have traveled across the world in search of it?

_____

5. A person who has done many good deeds in one life may be born as a rich and happy person in the next.

What word is not repeated after "next"?

_____

6. In ancient times, there were two great philosophies in China. One, Confucianism, was founded by a real historical person, Confucius. The other, Taoism, was believed to have been founded by a probably mythical figure called Lao-Tzu, a name which means "old master."

What were Confucianism and Taoism?

_____

7. Like Ptolemy, Copernicus worked out the details of orbital motion, but his worked better than Ptolemy's.

What did Copernicus's details of orbital motion work better than?

_____

Comprehension Questions

Answer the following questions by writing the answer on the blank lines or by circling **True** or **False** or the letter of the correct answer. If a statement is false, explain why it is false.

Paragraph 2

1. How have people looked for the edge of the universe for the last three hundred years?

    _____

Paragraph 3

2. What caused people's ideas about the universe to become more complicated?

    a. They traveled more.
    b. They learned more.
    c. They thought more about what they learned
    d. a, b, and c

3. What did people see about the planets, the sun, and the moon?

    _____

Paragraph 4

4. **True** or **False**   Aristotle and Aristarchus had the same ideas about the universe.

5. Whose ideas were right — Aristotle's or Aristarchus's?

    _____

Paragraph 6

6. **True** or **False**   Aristotle and Ptolemy had the same view of the universe.

7. In line 3, the words "this thinking" refer to

   a. Aristotle and Ptolemy.
   b. the Aristotelian or Ptolemaic view of the universe.
   c. popular in Europe for many hundreds of years.

Paragraph 7

8. **True** or **False**   Giordano Bruno believed that the universe had an edge.

Paragraph 8

9. **True** or **False**   Galileo invented the telescope.

10. Why did Galileo think that the planets were closer than the stars?

_____

11. **True** or **False**   The Milky Way is a river of mist.

Paragraph 9

12. **True** or **False**   Our sun is part of the Milky Way.

Paragraph 10

13. **True** or **False**   Our sun is in the center of the Milky Way galaxy.

Paragraph 11

14. If you travel at the speed of light, how long will it take you to reach Alpha Centauri?

_____

✎ Writing Assignment

Write a paragraph that includes the following:

- What did you already know before you read the reading selection?
- What did you learn from this reading that you did not know before?
- What would you like to learn more about?
- How can you learn more?

Within this spiral nebula, particles of matter are joining together to form stars.
Courtesy Mount Wilson and Palomar Observatories.

11 The Birth and Death of Stars

- What do you know about stars?
- What are they made of?
- How do stars begin?
- Do they have an end?
- Are there different kinds of stars?
- What is the nearest star to our earth?

Work with a partner or in small groups. On the map below, write information about stars under each heading. Do not write complete sentences. If you are not sure about something, make some guesses.

When everyone is finished, combine the information from each group on the board.

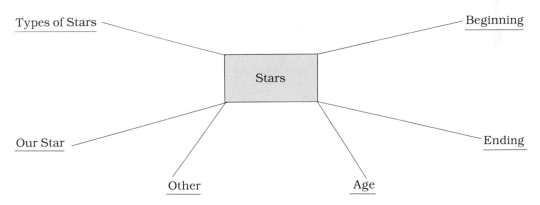

Types of Stars

Beginning

Stars

Our Star

Ending

Other

Age

In the following reading selection, a few scientific words are used that you need to be familiar with. Although the following are not truly scientific definitions, they will make the meanings somewhat clearer.

mass   quantity of matter. (See Chapter 5 for **matter**.) Matter occupies space and has mass. All objects with mass are attracted to all other objects with mass by gravity.

density   The quantity of mass in a certain volume of space. (See Chapter 10 for **dense**.) The higher the density of an object, the more mass is present in the same volume.

particle   A very small object, usually an atom or part of an atom such as a proton or an electron.

reaction   When something changes in such a way that something different is produced, we speak of a reaction occurring. For example, hydrogen reacts to form helium in a nuclear fusion reaction.

energy   Anything that can do work has energy. There are many kinds of energy. Moving objects have **kinetic** energy. Heat is a form of energy. Light is a form of **radiant** energy. There are other kinds of radiant energy such as microwaves and radio waves.

READING SELECTION

The Birth and Death of Stars

Bright star, would I were stedfast as thou art," wrote the poet John Keats, and, indeed, to most of us, stars are steadfast (unchanging). Modern astronomers have a different picture of the stars, however. Although the stars are not alive, they have a lifespan. They are born, they grow old, and eventually they die. They do not appear to change because they last a long time — millions to billions of years. Our sun is a star that is about five billion years old, and it will last about another five billion years.

(2)   Stars release tremendously large amounts of energy. It is for this reason that they are visible at great distances — billions of billions of miles and more. This great energy is released by reactions between the nuclei of the atoms that are within the stars.

(3)   All ordinary matter is made up of atoms. Atoms are extremely small. If a hundred thousand of them were lined up, the line would be no longer than the thickness of this piece of paper. An atom consists of a central, very massive, nucleus surrounded by lightweight particles called *electrons*. The diameter of an atom is ten thousand to one hundred thousand times greater than the diameter of the nucleus, but most of the mass of the atom is concentrated in the nucleus.

(4)   At ordinary temperatures, atoms react with each other chemically by transferring or sharing electrons. At very high temperatures (millions of degrees), the nuclei of atoms will combine together to form larger nuclei. This process is called nuclear *fusion*. (In nuclear *fission*, the atoms split apart.) Two of the most important factors in the development of stars are nuclear fusion and the law of gravity.

(5)   Because of the law of gravity, all material particles are attracted to each other. Large clumps of gaseous material called nebulae (singular = nebula) occur because of gravity. Within these nebulae, stars are often formed. Particles of matter inside the nebulae attract each other and are pulled together into a smaller and smaller volume, forming a star. Young stars are made up mostly of hydrogen atoms, the simplest and least massive of all atoms.

(6)   As the star shrinks in volume, the energy from gravity is changed to heat energy, and the temperature of the star rises. When the surface of the star reaches a temperature of about 2000 °C, the star begins to shine. The

shrinking continues until the center of the star reaches a temperature of a few million degrees. At this temperature, the hydrogen atoms in the star begin to combine to form helium atoms.

(7)   The fusion of hydrogen to form helium is a process that takes place in a large number of stars. Such stars are called *main sequence* stars. The larger the mass of the star, the higher is its temperature. Stars with higher temperatures shine more brightly. They also lose their hydrogen through fusion more rapidly. It will take our sun another five billion years to use up most of its hydrogen. Stars three times the mass of the sun will exhaust their hydrogen in a half billion years. Stars one half the mass of the sun will take two hundred billion years to do the same.

(8)   As the hydrogen gets used up, the central core of the star gets smaller and smaller, and its temperature rises to one hundred million degrees. This extremely high temperature causes the gases around the outside of the core to expand tremendously, and the star is then called a *red giant*. When our sun becomes a red giant (five billion years from now), the radius of its gases will extend out beyond the earth's orbit. The earth will then be swallowed up by the sun.

(9)   When the core of a star reaches a temperature of one hundred million degrees, the temperature is hot enough for a new kind of nuclear reaction to occur in the core. In this reaction, helium atoms combine to form larger atoms, starting with carbon and going on to oxygen and, in the case of the most massive of stars, to iron. The gases around the core continue to expand, and the star becomes a *red supergiant*, with a radius that might expand as far as Jupiter's orbit around the sun. At this point, energy is generated at a very high rate, and the star does not remain in this stage long.

(10) Because of the great energy production and high temperature of these supergiants, layers of gases are expelled from the core of the star until eventually only the core is left. In the case of low mass stars (such as our sun), this is the last stage of the star's lifetime. It is now about the size of a planet such as the earth, and it is called a *white dwarf*. A pint container of the material in a white dwarf would have a mass of 500 tons. White dwarfs cool until, eventually, they do not shine any more, and they float, cold and dark, through the universe.

(11) Not all stars become white dwarfs. The cores of more massive stars continue to shrink and go to higher and higher temperatures until eventually they are torn apart by tremendous explosions. In this explosive stage an amount of energy is given off that is equal to the energy ordinarily given off by a whole galaxy of one hundred billion stars. Such a star is called a *supernova*. The core that remains behind after the explosion is very small, about the size of a city such as New York, and is called a *neu-*

tron star. This star is one hundred million times the density of a white dwarf, and it gives off a great quantity of energy in the form of X-rays.

(12) Is there anything more dense than a neutron star? Apparently there is. Some very massive stars continue shrinking to a size less than that of a neutron star. As their density becomes greater and greater, it becomes more and more difficult for anything to escape from them. Finally, they reach a point at which even light can no longer escape. They are then called *black holes.* Their matter is so extremely dense that even light cannot escape. They cannot be seen, of course, because they do not give off any light. Nevertheless, astronomers believe they have detected a few because of the effect they have on the surrounding stars.

EXERCISES

Scanning Questions

Look back in the reading selection to find the answers to the following questions:

Paragraph 1

1. Why do stars not appear to change?

_____

Paragraph 2

2. Why are stars visible at great distances?

_____

3. How is energy from the stars released?

_____

Paragraph 3

4. What does an atom consist of?

_____

5. Where is most of the mass of the atom concentrated?

_____

Paragraph 4

6. How do atoms react with each other at ordinary temperatures?

_____

7. What happens to atoms at very high temperatures?

_____

Paragraph 5

8. How are stars formed inside a nebula?

_____

Paragraph 6

9. As the star shrinks in volume, what happens to the energy from gravity?

_____

10. What happens to the hydrogen atoms in the star at a temperature of a few million degrees?

_____

Paragraph 7

11. What kind of stars shine more brightly?

_____

12. How do stars lose hydrogen?

_____

Paragraph 8

13. What happens to stars as the hydrogen gets used up?

_____

14. What causes the gases around the outside of the core (of the star) to expand tremendously?

_____

Paragraph 9

15. What happens in the new kind of nuclear reaction?

_____

Paragraph 10

16. What causes layers of gases to be expelled from the core of the star until eventually only the core is left?

_____

17. What happens to white dwarf stars when they cool?

_____

Paragraph 11

18. What kind of stars do not become white dwarfs?

_____

19. In what form is the energy that a neutron star gives off?

_____

Paragraph 12

20. Why can't black holes be seen?

_____

Vocabulary

Fill in the blanks with the correct words from the list below. Sentence **a** of each pair of sentences is from the reading selection. Look back at the reading to help you. Sentence **b** of each pair uses the same word as sentence **a** with the same meaning.

amount(s)	process	share(-ing)	visible
energy	release(d)	transfer(ring)	

1a. Stars _____ tremendously large amounts of energy.

b. The little boy was holding a balloon. He opened his hand and

_____ the balloon. It went up in the air and disappeared.

2a. Stars release tremendously large _____ of energy.

b. When I was young and didn't have much money, ten dollars seemed

like a large _____ of money.

3a. It is for this reason that they are _____ at great distances — billions of billions of miles and more.

b. As he watched it sail away, the ship grew smaller and smaller on the

horizon until it was no longer _____.

4a. At ordinary temperatures, atoms react with each other chemically

by _____ or sharing electrons.

b. I don't have any money in my checking account, and I have some

bills to pay. I don't like _____ money from my savings account to my checking account, but I have to, or I will not be able to pay my bills on time.

5a. At ordinary temperatures, atoms react with each other chemically

by transferring or _____ electrons.

b. The two children are very good at _____ things. If one
of them gets a piece of candy, he breaks it in two pieces and gives
one of the pieces to his brother.

6a. As the star shrinks in volume, the _____ from gravity

is changed to heat _____, and the temperature of the
star rises.

b. Heat and light have _____ and can be made to do
work.

7a. The fusion of hydrogen to form helium is a _____ that
takes place in a large number of stars.

b. I like the way my hair looks when it has been cut, but I dislike the

_____ of having it cut.

Do the same with the following:

    core   exhaust   expel(led)   quantity
    effect(s)   expand(s)   generate(d)

8a. Stars three times the mass of the sun will _____ their
hydrogen in a half billion years.

b. I have $12.00, and I won't get paid for four days. I can spend only

$3.00 per day. If I spend more than that, I will _____
my money before pay day.

9a. As the hydrogen gets used up, the central _____ of
the star gets smaller and smaller, and its temperature rises to one
hundred million degrees.

b. When we have eaten the good part of an apple, the

_____ with the seeds and the stem is left.

10a. This extremely high temperature causes the gases around the out-

side of the core to _____ tremendously, and the star is then called a *red giant*.

 b. When there isn't any air in a balloon, it is very small and flat. When

you blow air into the balloon, it _____ and gets much bigger.

11a. At this point, energy is _____ at a very high rate, and the star does not remain in this stage long.

 b. I had to write a 2,000-word essay in four hours. I had to

_____ five hundred words per hour. I wasn't sure that I could produce that many words every hour!

12a. Because of the great energy production and high temperature of

these supergiants, layers of gases are _____ from the core of the star until eventually only the core is left.

 b. When I pricked a hole in the balloon, air was _____ from the hole as the balloon collapsed.

13a. This star is one hundred million times the density of a white dwarf,

and it gives off a great _____ of energy in the form of X-rays.

 b. A pint of water weighs one pound. One pound of water is the same

_____ of water as one pint of water.

14a. Nevertheless, astronomers believe they have detected a few be-

cause of the _____ they have on the surrounding stars.

 b. Alcohol has a terrible _____ on a person's ability to drive. No one who has been drinking should drive.

Self-Test

Fill in the blanks with the correct words from the list below.

amount	energy	expelled	quantity	transfer
core	exhausted	generate	release	visible
effects	expand	process	sharing	

1. Automobiles _____ a lot of oxides of nitrogen and carbon monoxide into the air, which causes air pollution.

2. He thought that I could not see him, but he was clearly

   _____ where he was trying to hide behind a tree.

3. I wrote a long composition. I _____ everything I had to say about the topic.

4. The two monkeys had to get used to _____ their cage with each other. It was not possible to put them in separate cages.

5. A million grains of sand is only a small _____ of all the sand on a beach.

6. A lot of the _____ we use every day comes to our homes in the form of electricity.

7. The _____ of building a house is complex. Many different skills are needed.

8. When Americans eat, they _____ their forks from their left hands to their right hands after they cut their meat.

9. Dams can be used to _____ a lot of electrical energy.

10. One of the _____ of air pollution is acid rain.

11. Deep inside the earth there is a dense _____ made of iron and nickel.

12. It is the gas that is _____ from the back of a rocket that makes the rocket go forward.

13. There is a large _____ of books in a library.

14. Heat causes metals to _____. Cold makes them get smaller.

Organization

Paragraphs 5 through 10 of the Reading Selection describe the process that occurs from the formation of a star as a main sequence star to its end as a white dwarf. This process can be divided into five stages.

Below are groups of details from paragraphs 5 through 10 that describe the five stages. Read each group of details and decide which stage each group belongs to. The details of the first stage have been marked. Mark the other groups with 2, 3, 4, or 5.

_____   gases are expelled, only the core is left, it does not shine

___1___   particles inside a nebula are attracted to each other, they are pulled together to make a smaller and smaller volume, eventually a young star is formed

_____   at 100,000,000° there is a new kind of nuclear reaction in the core, helium atoms combine to form larger atoms, gases continue to expand

_____   as hydrogen gets used up the central core of the star gets smaller, temperature rises to 100,000,000°, gases expand

_____   the star shrinks, energy from gravity is changed to heat energy, shrinking continues until the center of the star is a few million degrees, hydrogen atoms begin to combine to form helium atoms

The stars in stages 3, 4, and 5 are called by specific names. Write the name for each stage.

3 _____   4 _____   5 _____

Inference

Sometimes an idea or some information is not directly stated in a reading, but we can **infer** this information from what is directly stated.

⮕ *Example*

Mrs. Jones put on her rain coat and rain hat and picked up her umbrella before she went out.

Knowledge: Mrs. Jones is wearing a rain coat and a rain hat. She has an umbrella. She has gone out.

Inference: It is raining.

No knowledge   We do not have any information about where Mrs. *or information:* Jones is going.

Below are some sentences that contain inferences. There are three choices after each sentence or group of sentences. One of the choices is something that we can infer. Put a check (✔) on the line in front of the inference.

⮕ *Example*

If it rains tomorrow, we can't have the picnic.

_____ **a.** It is going to rain tomorrow.
_____ **b.** We like picnics.
___✔___ **c.** We are planning to have a picnic tomorrow.

a is incorrect.   We do not know that it is going to rain tomorrow. It is only a possibility.

b is incorrect.   There is no information about our feelings toward picnics. Maybe we will be happy if it rains tomorrow because we do not like picnics!

c is the inference.

1. Mary's cat gave birth to kittens yesterday.

    _____ **a.** Mary has a cat.
    _____ **b.** Mary's cat is a female.
    _____ **c.** There were six kittens.

2. There was an earthquake that destroyed many houses last week.

    _____ **a.** There was an earthquake last week.
    _____ **b.** Many people were killed.
    _____ **c.** Many people were homeless after the earthquake.

3. There is too much snow in this part of the country in the winter. I am not used to so much snow.

    _____ **a.** I am not from this part of the country.
    _____ **b.** I like snow.
    _____ **c.** It snows a lot here in the winter.

4. John remembered to feed the cat.

    _____ **a.** John was supposed to feed the cat.
    _____ **b.** John fed the cat.
    _____ **c.** The cat is black.

5. If I win a million dollars in the lottery, I will travel around the world.

    _____ **a.** I won a million dollars.
    _____ **b.** I am going to travel around the world.
    _____ **c.** I bought a lottery ticket.

6. The mother gave the little boy his lunch in a paper bag when he left for school.
    _____ **a.** The little boy has a paper bag with his lunch in it.
    _____ **b.** The mother made the lunch.
    _____ **c.** The little boy is probably not going to eat lunch at home.

7. You cannot graduate from this university until you pass the language exam. Mary graduated last June.

    _____ **a.** Mary passed the language exam.
    _____ **b.** Mary has graduated.
    _____ **c.** The language exam is difficult.

8. Our baseball team finally won a game.

    _____ **a.** We have a baseball team.

    _____ **b.** Until now, our baseball team has not won a game for a long time.

    _____ **c.** Our school also has a soccer team.

9. I like my new car better than my old car. My old car did not have front-wheel drive.

    _____ **a.** I have two cars.

    _____ **b.** I like my new car better than my old car.

    _____ **c.** My new car has front-wheel drive.

10. It is nice to take flowers when you are invited to someone's house for dinner. We took flowers to the Smiths last week.

    _____ **a.** The Smiths like flowers.

    _____ **b.** We were invited to dinner at the Smiths' house last week.

    _____ **c.** Flowers are nice.

Comprehension Questions

Answer the following questions by circling **True** or **False** or the letter of the correct answer, or by writing the answer on the blank lines. If a statement is false, explain why it is false.

Paragraph 2

1. **True** or **False**   We can see the stars at great distances because they release tremendous amounts of energy.

Paragraph 4

2. What happens in nuclear fusion?

_____

Paragraph 5

3. Why do particles of matter inside nebulae attract each other and get pulled together into smaller and smaller volume?

_____

Paragraph 6

4. **True** or **False**   The star stops shrinking when its surface reaches a temperature of about 2,000°.

5. At what temperature do the hydrogen atoms in a star begin to combine to form helium atoms?

_____

Paragraph 7

6. **True** or **False**   Stars with a large mass use up their hydrogen faster than stars with a smaller mass do.

Paragraph 8

7. As the hydrogen gets used up

   a. the central core of the star and the area of gases around the outside of the core both get smaller.
   b. the central core of the star gets smaller, but the area of gases around the outside of the core gets larger.
   c. the central core of the star gets smaller, but the area of gases around the outside of the core stays the same size.

Paragraph 9

8. What temperature is required for helium atoms to combine to form larger atoms?

   _____

Paragraph 10

9. **True** or **False**   The last stage of a low mass star's lifetime comes when all the gases have been expelled from the core.

Paragraph 11

10. **True** or **False**   A neutron star gives off energy in the form of X-rays.

✍ Writing Assignment

Read each paragraph again and write one question for each paragraph.

After you write your questions, find a partner. Ask each other the questions that you wrote.

Look at the Reading Selection to find the answers to your partner's questions. Answer the questions orally. Do not write the answers.

As the train races by, sound waves move to create the Doppler effect.
Courtesy of Baltimore & Ohio Railroad.

12 The Fate of the Universe

In Chapter 11 we discussed the beginning and ending of stars in the universe. In Chapter 12 we will discuss whether or not the universe had a beginning or will have an ending.

Below are some statements about the universe. Read each statement and decide if you agree or disagree with it. Draw a circle around the word **Agree** or the word **Disagree** after each statement. This is not a test! Use your own knowledge or your own opinion or make a guess.

1. The universe has always existed and will always exist.   Agree   Disagree
2. The universe began with an explosion.   Agree   Disagree
3. Other galaxies are moving away from us.   Agree   Disagree
4. The universe is expanding.   Agree   Disagree
5. The universe is getting smaller.   Agree   Disagree
6. The universe is staying the same size.   Agree   Disagree
7. The universe will continue to expand forever.   Agree   Disagree
8. The universe will stay the same size forever.   Agree   Disagree
9. The universe will get smaller and smaller until it almost disappears.   Agree   Disagree
10. If number 9 happens, the universe will begin to expand again.   Agree   Disagree

When you finish, compare your answers with those of some of your classmates.

READING SELECTION

The Fate of the Universe

T he man with the spear at the edge of the universe was looking for an end — or a beginning — of the universe in space. People have also speculated about the beginning or the end of the universe in time. Most early cultures had a creation story, a story of how the earth came to be. Until recently, many scientists believed that the universe extends outward in all directions and that it has always been and will always be. Discoveries in the twentieth century, however, have changed the way scientists think about the universe.

(2) Nowadays, there are fewer trains than there used to be and just about all of them are electric. In the days of steam locomotives, however, you could stand by the railroad tracks and listen to the whistle of the locomotive as the train went by. As the train approached, the sound of the whistle would be high pitched. After it passed, the pitch changed and the sound was lower pitched. This also sometimes happens when you pass a large truck going in the opposite direction on a highway. This change in pitch of sound emitted by a moving object is called the *Doppler effect* and it happens with all sorts of wave motion.

(3) The Doppler effect is also observed with light and with radiant energy in general. In light, the color changes instead of sound. When objects are moving toward us, the color of their light shifts toward blue or violet. When objects are moving away from us, the color of their light shifts toward red. Because light travels so much more rapidly than sound, objects must be traveling much faster than a speeding locomotive before the Doppler effect is observed with light.

(4) A twentieth-century American astronomer called Hubble — the man for whom the space telescope is named — studied the light from galaxies other than ours and made some interesting discoveries. He found that the light of all other galaxies was shifted toward the red. All the other galaxies were moving away from ours. Furthermore, the farther away these galaxies were from us, the faster they were moving. It seems as if we are in the center of a universe in which everything else is trying to get away from us.

(5) We believe that what is really happening is that space itself is expanding. A balloon is a good analogy. Suppose we didn't live on the surface of the earth but on the surface of a balloon that was being blown up.

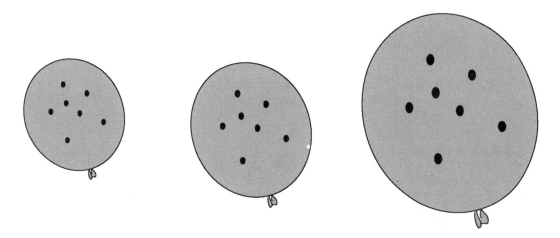

The dots represent people on the balloon's surface. It would appear to us that everyone else was moving away from us, and everyone else would have the same feeling. However, what is really happening is that the balloon is getting bigger.

(6)   If the universe is expanding, then in the past it must have been smaller than it is now. Far back in the past it must, in fact, have been only a tiny point. Scientists believe that the universe began its expansion about fifteen billion years ago. (Because of various uncertainties it could be anywhere between twelve and twenty billion years ago.) This theory of the beginning of the universe is often called the "big bang" theory. However, it was not the kind of explosion in which matter flies out into space. It is space itself (the three-dimensional universe) that is expanding.

(7)   Once we know that the universe is expanding, another interesting question occurs to us: Is the universe going to go on expanding forever or will it slow down and some day stop? There are three possibilities: (1) the universe will expand forever without slowing down, (2) the expansion will slow down and stop, and the universe will then contract, getting smaller and smaller, and (3) it will continue to expand, but more and more slowly, never quite coming to a stop. The first possibility would eventually result in groups of galaxies that are completely isolated from one another and it would be a rather lonely universe. In the second possibility, at some point the universe would shrink to the same almost nonexistent point that it was before the big bang. This might be followed by another big bang. The third possibility would result in what is called a flat universe — the expansion will become slower and slower without ever completely coming to a stop. If this happens, the universe would continue to be similar to what it is now.

(8)   We do not know which one of these three possibilities will happen because the answer lies in the density of the universe, which we do not

know accurately enough. The more dense the universe is — that is, the more matter there is on the average in a volume of space — the more likely it is that the universe will contract because of the gravitational force. If the density is just right, the universe will be "flat." If the density is higher than this "just right" density, the universe will collapse at some time in the future. If the density is lower, the universe will go on expanding forever. We know the density of the universe is very close to the "just right" density, but we don't know it accurately enough to determine among the three possibilities.

EXERCISES

Scanning Questions

Look back at the reading selection to find the answers to the following questions:

Paragraph 1

1. What did many scientists believe about the universe until recently?

_____

Paragraph 2

2. As the train approached, was the sound low pitched or high pitched?

_____

3. When was the sound lower pitched?

_____

4. What is the Doppler effect?

_____

Paragraph 3

5. In the Doppler effect with light, what changes instead of sound?

_____

6. When does the color of an object shift toward blue or violet?

_____

7. When does the color of an object shift toward red?

_____

Paragraph 4

8. What did Hubble discover about the light of all the galaxies other than ours?

_____

9. What were all the other galaxies doing?

_____

Paragraph 5

10. What do we believe is really happening?

_____

Paragraph 6

11. What must the universe have been far back in the past?

_____

12. When do scientists believe the universe began its expansion?

_____

13. What is this theory of the beginning of the universe called?

_____

Paragraph 7

14. What would the first possibility result in?

_____

15. What would happen to the universe in the second possibility?

_____

16. What happens (to expansion) in a flat universe?

_____

Paragraph 8

17. Why don't we know which one of these three possibilities will happen?

_____

18. What will happen to the universe if the density is just right?

_____

19. What will happen if the density is higher than this "just right"?

_____

20. What will happen if the density is lower than "just right"?

_____

Vocabulary

Fill in the blanks with the correct words from the list below. Sentence **a** of each pair is from the reading selection. Sentence **b** of each pair uses the same word as sentence **a** with the same meaning.

> analogy   recently   speculate(d)
> emit(ted)   shift(s)

1a. People have also _____ about the beginning or the end of the universe in time.

b. The two police officers _____ about who the killer could be, but neither of them had a good guess.

2a. Until _____, many scientists believed that the universe extends outward in all directions and that it has always been and will always be.

b. "I've been to that restaurant _____," she said. "I'd rather go somewhere I haven't been to for a while."

3a. This change in pitch of sound _____ by a moving object is called the *Doppler effect* and it happens with all sorts of wave motion.

b. The truck _____ a lot of black smoke from its exhaust pipe, making it a great source of air pollution.

4a. When objects are moving toward us, the color of their light

_____ toward blue or violet.

b. Americans hold their forks in their left hands when they cut their

meat. Then they _____ the fork to their right hands to eat.

5a. A balloon is a good _____.

b. An ant hill can serve as an _____ for a city. It is like a city in many ways. A very large number of ants live in an ant hill, there is a lot of construction, and the ants cooperate to achieve goals just as people do.

Do the same with the following:

collapse   lonely   similar
contract   non-existent

6a. There are three possibilities: (1) the universe will expand forever without slowing down, (2) the expansion will slow down and stop,

and the universe will then _____, getting smaller and smaller, and (3) it will continue to expand, but more and more slowly, never quite coming to a stop.

b. The opposite of *expand* is _____.

7a. The first possibility would eventually result in groups of galaxies that are completely isolated from one another and it would be a

rather _____ universe.

b. The little boy had no one to play with. He felt very

_____.

8a. In the second possibility, at some point the universe would shrink to

the same almost _____ point that it was before the big bang.

b. Some children believe in Santa Claus, but when they get older, they

realize that he is _____.

9a. If this happens, the universe would continue to be

_____ to what it is now.

b. When you looked at the two girls, they appeared to be

_____. They were about the same height, they both
had blonde hair, and their noses were the same shape.

10a. If the density is higher than this "just right" density, the universe

will _____ at some time in the future.

b. That chair does not look very strong. I'm afraid it will

_____ if I stand on it.

Self-Test

Fill in the blanks with the correct words from the list below.

analogy	contract	lonely	recently	similar
collapse	emitted	nonexistent	shift	speculate

1. It is the material that is _____ from the back of a rocket
   that pushes the rocket forward.

2. We don't know what will happen in the future, but many people like

   to _____ about it.

3. A bridge is often used as an _____ for life. One shore
   represents birth, and the other shore represents death or the afterlife.
   The bridge itself represents our lifespan between birth and death.

4. When they are in danger, turtles will _____ by pulling
   their heads and feet in under their shell.

5. The house was a very ordinary house. It was _____ to
   many others that she had seen.

6. "How _____ have you seen him?" I asked. "I saw him
   just a few days ago," she answered.

7. He was so old that all of his friends had died. He felt very

   _____.

8. Building a house out of playing cards has to be done very carefully or

   it will _____.

9. I am tired of riding in the back seat. If you will _____ from the front seat to the back, then I will be able to sit up front for a while.

10. Over five billion years ago, when the earth was just formed, life on

    earth was _____. It was probably about two billion years later that life began.

Organization: Topics and Details

Below are some groups of sentences. In each group, one sentence is a topic sentence, and the other two sentences are details about the topic. Write **T** on the line in front of each topic sentence. Write **D** on the line in front of each detail.

⟫ *Example*

      _____ **a.** One shore represents life, and the other shore represents death or the afterlife.
      _____ **b.** The bridge itself represents our lifespan between birth and death.
      _____ **c.** A bridge is often used as an analogy for life.

The topic is **c**. Write a **T** on the line in front of **c**. The other two sentences explain how a bridge is an analogy for life. Write a **D** on the lines in front of **a** and **b**.

1. _____ a. Stars are born.
   _____ b. Stars have a lifespan.
   _____ c. Stars grow old and eventually die.

2. _____ a. As the train approached, the sound of the whistle was high pitched.
   _____ b. After the train passed, the sound was lower pitched.
   _____ c. The change in pitch of sound emitted by a moving object is called the Doppler effect.

3. _____ a. When objects are moving toward us, the color of their light shifts toward blue or violet.
   _____ b. When objects are moving away from us, the color of their light shifts toward red.
   _____ c. In light, the color changes instead of sound.

Text Mapping

On the next page is a text map for paragraph 7 of the Reading Selection. Write the correct sentence or part of a sentence from Chapter 7 in each box on the map. Three have been done for you.

Topic

Is the universe going to go on expanding forever, or will it slow
down and some day stop?

Possibilities

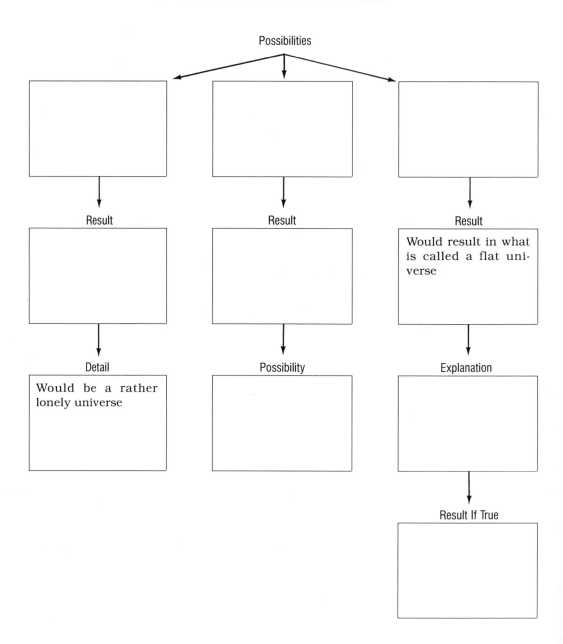

Result

Result

Result

Would result in what
is called a flat uni-
verse

Detail

Possibility

Explanation

Would be a rather
lonely universe

Result If True

Synonyms

Below are a list of ten words and seven sentences with an underlined word in each sentence.
    Cross out (X) the underlined word in each sentence and replace it with the correct synonym from the list. There are three words in the list that you cannot use.

accurate	contrary	generate	origin	similar to
center	core	location	quantity	speculate

1. Nuclear power plants use uranium to <u>produce</u> electricity.

2. The recipe for this cake requires a large <u>amount</u> of butter.

3. The city finally decided on a <u>site</u> for the new library.
   They are going to build it near the school.

4. My husband and I have <u>opposite</u> views as to where we want to live.
   He wants to live in the country, but I want to live in the city.

5. It is not possible for us to know what the future will be for us. We can only <u>guess</u> about it.

6. The <u>beginning</u> of human speech is unknown.

7. A dog is not <u>like</u> a cat.

Antonyms

Below is a list of ten words followed by eight sentences. In each sentence, one word is used incorrectly for the meaning of the sentence. Look at each sentence and decide which word is incorrect.

From the list, find the antonym for each incorrect word that is correct for the meaning of the sentence. Rewrite each sentence correctly.

The first one is done for you. There are two words that you cannot use.

accurate	dissimilar	expand	float	regular
certain	empty	famous	nonexistent	unusual

1. Oranges and bananas are similar.

   (The incorrect word is <u>similar</u>.)

   Oranges and bananas are dissimilar.

   (The antonym of similar is <u>dissimilar</u>. Now sentence makes sense.)

2. A car cannot function with a full gas tank.

   _____

3. Heat makes metals contract.

   _____

4. A piece of wood will sink if you put it in the water.

   _____

5. Popular movie actors are unknown.

   _____

6. The sun is irregular in its movements.

   _____

7. It is unsure that the sun will rise tomorrow.

_____

8. This is a very good watch. It keeps very incorrect time.

_____

Word Families

Listed below are different forms of some of the vocabulary words in Chapters 10, 11, and 12.
The new forms are different parts of speech. Study them before you do the exercise.

Verbs	Nouns	Adjectives	Adverbs
center	center	central	centrally
effect	effect	(in)effective	effectively
expand	expansion	expanded	——
extend	extension	extended	
		extensive	extensively
		recent	recently
——	similarity	(dis)similar	——
speculate	speculation	speculative	——

1. centered   center   central   centrally

   a. The post office has a _____ location right in the
      middle of the town.

   b. There is a lot of iron and other metals at the earth's

      _____.

   c. She wasn't satisfied until she _____ the vase ex-
      actly in the middle of the table.

   d. To be successful, a hotel should be _____ located.

2. effect   effects   effective   ineffective   effectively

    a. He was very _____ at his job and his boss was
pleased.

    b. One of the possible _____ of smoking is lung
cancer.

    c. The students wanted to _____ some changes at the
university, so they went to the president's office to talk to him.

    d. Although he got along well with people, he was completely

    _____ in getting them to do what he wanted. He
did not make a good leader.

    e. He knew that in order to do his job _____ he would
have to work hard.

3. expand   expansion   expanded

Metals will _____ when the temperature rises. The
thermostat that controls a furnace makes use of this

_____ of metals when it is heated. When the tempera-

ture rises, the _____ metal in the thermostat makes an
electrical contact that turns off the furnace.

4. extend   extension   extended   extensive   extensively

    a. The park was very _____, with space for many
flower gardens and trees.

    b. The garage was an _____ of the house. A door of the
house opened right into the garage.

    c. He had traveled _____ in Canada and felt that he
knew a lot about Canadians.

    d. I tried to _____ my arm as far as possible so that I
could touch the ceiling.

    e. It was an _____ visit to Japan. We had a good time, and we stayed for six months.

5. recent   recently

    a. It was a _____ newspaper that he was holding. It was only two days old.

    b. _____, he seems to have become much nicer than he used to be.

6. similarity   similar   dissimilar

    a. Although they were sisters, they were very _____ in appearance. One was short and blonde. The other was tall and dark-haired.

    b. There isn't much _____ between chess and checkers except that they are played on the same kind of board.

    c. A leopard is _____ to a cat in everything but size. It looks just like a very big cat.

7. speculate   speculation   speculative

    a. There was a lot of _____ talk about where the treasure might be buried, but no one really knew.

    b. "It would be wrong to _____ about who committed the robbery," the detective said. "It could hurt an innocent person's reputation."

    c. I think philosophy is mostly _____ about things that no one can prove.

Comprehension Questions

Answer the following questions by circling **True** or **False** or the letter of the correct answer, or by writing the answer on the blank lines. If a statement is false, explain why it is false.

Paragraph 1

1. In line 8, the word *however* signals a contrast. What is the contrast?

   a. between the beginning or end of the universe in space and the beginning or end of the universe in time
   b. between early cultures' creation stories and modern knowledge
   c. between what scientists used to believe about the universe in space and time and what scientists think about it now?

Paragraph 2

2. **True** or **False**   Sound is a wave motion.

Paragraph 3

3. **True** or **False**   Light is a specific example of radiant energy.

Paragraph 4

4. How did Hubble know that all other galaxies were moving away from us?

   _____

Paragraph 5

5. What is a balloon a good analogy for?

   a. to explain how space is expanding
   b. to explain why it appears to us that the galaxies are moving away from us
   c. both **a** and **b**

Paragraph 6

6. **True** or **False**   The universe began with a big explosion that sent matter out into space.

Paragraph 7

7. What will eventually happen to the universe?

   a. It will go on expanding forever.
   b. It will some day slow down and stop.
   c. We are not certain.

8. In which one of the three possibilities in this paragraph will the universe continue to be similar to what it is now? (Your answer should be a number.)

Paragraph 8

9. Why don't we know which one of the three possibilities in paragraph 7 will happen?

   a. because the answer lies in the density of the universe
   b. because we do not know the density of the universe accurately enough to predict what will happen
   c. because the universe is very dense

10. **True** or **False**   Which one of the three possibilities is true depends on the density of the universe.

✐ Writing Assignment

Look back at your answers in the Pre-Reading Discussion on page 219. Have you changed your mind about any of your answers?
   Write a paragraph that includes the following:

- What did you already know before you read the reading selection?
- What did you learn from this reading that you did not know before?
- What would you like to learn more about? How can you learn more?

Chikamatsu Monzaemon, the renowned Japanese playwright, is
best known for his *joruri*, plays for the puppet theater. *Courtesy of
Japan National Tourist Organization.*

13 | Chikamatsu Monzaemon

In small groups, discuss the following:

- Who are some famous living authors in your country?
- Which one is your favorite? Why?
- What kinds of things does he or she write?
- Do you think that any of these writers will still be famous 100 years in the future? Why?

The English playwright William Shakespeare lived 400 years ago. However, he is still very famous. People still read his plays with great pleasure because they deal with human emotions and human conditions that are timeless.

- Is there an author from your country who has been dead at least one hundred years but whose writings are still popular?
- What did he or she write?
- Why are the writings still popular?

READING SELECTION

Chikamatsu Monzaemon

C hikamatsu Monzaemon was a Japanese writer of plays who lived from 1653 to 1715. Chikamatsu is still very famous in Japan for the plays that he wrote, and as a result he has sometimes been called the Japanese Shakespeare. Not only was he well known in his time and times afterward, but he also influenced many of the playwrights that followed him. He was one of the world's great playwrights.

(2)   There have been a number of types of theater in Japan. *No* plays, among the earliest, often had themes from Zen Buddhism and had very little in the way of scenery or attempts at realism. *No* plays are still performed, but no new ones have been written since the sixteenth century. *Kabuki* is the popular theater, with themes of greater human interest and with elaborate costumes and stage sets. Chikamatsu wrote some plays for the Kabuki theater, but his best plays were *joruri*, plays for the puppet theater. Although it may strike Westerners as strange that serious drama should use puppets as actors, in Japan it was taken very seriously.

(3)   Chikamatsu was born to *samurai* parents. The *samurai* were a class of warrior aristocrats who served a master. When Chikamatsu was still quite young, his father had become a *ronin*, that is, a *samurai* without a master. As Japan was somewhat crowded with *samurai* at this time, Chikamatsu would not have had much opportunity for success in trying to have a career as one. Instead, he became acquainted with the theater in the course of doing errands for an aristocratic friend of his, and he began writing plays.

(4)   In 1683, a puppet play that was probably his first was performed, and it was quite successful. In one part of the play, there was a scene in which someone's head was chopped off. This would, of course, be impossible with live actors, but it can be done with puppets. One of the advantages of *joruri* was that scenes of bloodshed or the supernatural that were impossible for live actors could be portrayed by puppets.

(5)   Relatively little is known of Chikamatsu's life except that he was enormously successful and undoubtedly made a good deal of money. Although he wrote for the puppet theater initially, from 1688 to 1703 he wrote mostly for Kabuki. Everyone agrees, however, that his Kabuki plays are not as good as his puppet plays. In 1703 he went back to writing *joruri* with a play called *The Love Suicides at Sonezaki*. Like most of Chikamat-

su's *joruri* plays, it was based on a contemporary incident that had occurred within the previous month or two. At this time, there was a craze for love suicides, mutual suicides of a man and a woman whose plans for a life together had been so frustrated that life did not seem worth living. This may have been reinforced by a popular religious belief that lovers who died together would be born together in Paradise. Chikamatsu's play concerned the love suicide of a shop clerk and the woman whom he wanted to marry but could not because his mother wanted him to marry another woman. It was very successful. It was in fact so successful that it saved the theater where it was performed from bankruptcy.

(6) Chikamatsu wrote many other puppet plays, including several others about love suicides. His plays were full of references to current events, and to actors, theaters, and teahouses of the time. In spite of this, his plays have lasted until the present day and are interesting to read in translation. (Shakespeare too made contemporary references, which today we simply pass over.) Because the plays usually dealt with very recent events, they have been called "living newspapers." A more modern idea of this might be "tubeless television" as *joruri* could be regarded as equivalent to the in-depth news coverage that we sometimes get on television.

(7) Many of Chikamatsu's plays deal with the conflict between *giri*, obligation or duty, and *ninjo*, human feeling. Although the Japanese had a strong sense of obligation to their parents and to society, they also had a strong desire for human happiness. When the conflict between them was such that human happiness seemed impossible, suicide was sometimes the answer.

(8) One of the most famous puppet plays of all time was written about fifty years after Chikamatsu's death by a combination of three playwrights who had been influenced by him. Called *Chusingara* or the *Treasury of Loyal Retainers*, it concerned an incident that had happened some time before and had been depicted in short plays by Chikamatsu and several of his rivals at that time. The story begins when one nobleman insults another in such a way that the insulted person feels he must commit suicide. His forty-seven *samurai* (now *ronin* or *samurai* without a master) swear to avenge him by killing the man who forced him to suicide. After a wait of several years, in which everyone is lulled into feeling that nothing will happen, they invade the nobleman's house and kill him. Because avenging their master is a crime, the play ends with the forty-seven *ronin* committing suicide.

(9) This play is also about *giri* or duty. The duty of the forty-seven *ronin* to their dead master is to avenge him. Their duty to the country and its ruler, the shogun, is to not commit private acts of vengeance. The *ronin* fulfill the first duty and then punish themselves with suicide for failing in the second duty.

EXERCISES

Scanning Questions

Look back at the reading selection to find the answers to the following questions:

Paragraph 1

1. When did Chikamatsu live?

_____

2. Why has Chikamatsu sometimes been called the Japanese Shakespeare?

_____

Paragraph 2

3. What are three types of Japanese theater that are mentioned in this paragraph?

_____

4. What were *joruri*?

_____

Paragraph 3

5. What were the *samurai*?

_____

6. What is a *ronin*?

_____

Paragraph 4

7. What would be impossible with live actors but can be done with puppets?

_____

Paragraph 5

8. What was *The Love Suicides at Sonezaki* based on?

_____

Paragraph 6

9. What were Chikamatsu's plays full of references to?

_____

10. Why have his plays been called "living newspapers?"

_____

11. What could *joruri* be regarded as equivalent to?

_____

Paragraph 7

12. What do many of Chikamatsu's plays deal with?

_____

Paragraph 8

13. Who wrote *Chusingara* or *The Treasury of Loyal Retainers*?

_____

14. When does the story (*Chusingara*) begin?

_____

15. How do his forty-seven *samurai* swear to avenge him?

_____

16. Why do the forty-seven *ronin* commit suicide?

_____

Paragraph 9

17. What is the duty of the forty-seven *ronin* to their dead master?

_____

18. What is the duty of the forty-seven *ronin* to the country and its ruler, the shogun?

_____

Vocabulary

Fill in the blank lines with the correct words from the list below. Remember, sentence **a** is from the reading selection. Sentence **b** of each pair uses the same word as sentence **a** with the same meaning.

advantage(s)	frustrate(d)	reinforce(d)	theme(s)
contemporary	realism	serious	

1a. *No* plays, among the earliest, often had _____ from Zen Buddhism and had very little in the way of scenery or attempts at realism.

b. The _____ of the science meeting was that of science helping society.

2a. *No* plays, among the earliest, often had themes from Zen Buddhism and had very little in the way of scenery or attempts at

_____.

b. His stories described the city with a great deal of accuracy. They

were well known for their _____.

3a. Although it may strike Westerners as strange that

_____ drama should use puppets as actors, in Japan
it was taken very seriously.

b. This was not a story that would make people laugh. It was a

_____ story.

4a. One of the _____ of *joruri* was that scenes of bloodshed or the supernatural that were impossible for live actors could
be portrayed by puppets.

b. Being tall is a great _____ if you're trying to reach

something up high. It is not an _____ in a house with
low ceilings.

5a. Like most of Chikamatsu's *joruri* plays, it was based on a

_____ incident that had occurred within the previous
month or two.

b. _____ history is the history of very recent times —
what is occurring right now.

6a. At this time, there was a craze for love suicides, mutual suicides of a
man and a woman whose plans for a life together had been so

_____ that life did not seem worth living.

b. I wanted to go on a picnic, but the rain had _____ my
plans and I was unable to go.

7a. This may have been _____ by a popular religious belief that lovers who died together would be born together in Paradise.

b. I believed his story. Two other people had said almost the same

thing and that _____ what he had said.

Do the same with the following:

conflict	fail(ing)	invade(d)	reference(s)
depict(ed)	force(d)	lulled	

8a. His plays were full of _____ to current events, and to actors, theaters and teahouses of the time.

b. They had both spent some time in Paris and their conversation was

filled with _____ to streets and places that I did not know.

9a. Many of Chikamatsu's plays deal with the _____ between *giri*, obligation or duty, and *ninjo*, human feeling.

b. I want to take these two classes, but their times _____. One is from 11:00 to 11:50, and the other is from 11:30 to 1:00.

10a. Called *Chusingara* or the *Treasury of Loyal Retainers*, it concerned an incident that had happened some time before and had been

_____ in short plays by Chikamatsu and several of his rivals at that time.

b. The painting _____ the inside of a vegetable store. It was a very realistic picture of the store. The vegetables looked very realistic.

11a. His forty-seven *samurai* (now *ronin* or *samurai* without a master)

swear to avenge him by killing the man who _____ him to suicide.

b. His parents _____ him to do his homework even though he didn't want to.

12a. After a wait of several years, in which everyone is

_____ into feeling that nothing will happen, they invade the nobleman's house and kill him.

b. The tiger looked so soft and gentle that the man was

_____ into thinking that the tiger wouldn't harm him.

13a. After a wait of several years, in which everyone is lulled into feeling

that nothing will happen, they _____ the nobleman's house and kill him.

b. No foreign soldiers have marched into England for many years. In

other words, England has not been _____ for a long time.

14a. The *ronin* fulfill the first duty and then punish themselves with sui-

cide for _____ in the second duty.

b. She didn't seem to understand what he was talking about. He knew

he was _____ to explain the lesson to her.

Self-Test

Fill in the blank lines with the correct words from the following:

advantage	depicts	frustrated	realism	serious
conflict	failing	invade	references	theme
contemporary	forced	lull	reinforce	

1. The Dutch painters of the sixteenth and seventeenth centuries painted pictures of objects so true to life that you feel you can reach out and touch them. These painters were masters of the art of

_____.

2. They had been given a choice of five subjects for their paper and he

   had a difficult time deciding on the _____ he wanted to
   write about.

3. Being on a hill was an _____ for a castle. It made it
   difficult for the enemy to capture it.

4. No matter how many times he tried to draw a dog, it looked like a cat.

   He was very _____.

5. The doctors in the operating room were very _____.
   They were afraid the patient might die.

6. Magazines   and   newspaper   are   written   mostly   about

   _____ happenings — things that are going on right
   now.

7. Some parents give their children a reward to _____
   good behavior.

8. Every time one brother wanted something, the other brother wanted

   the same thing. There always seemed to be a _____
   between them.

9. She was rocking the baby while she sang to it, trying to

   _____ it back to sleep.

10. He made several _____ to his big house and his new
    car. He was trying to impress us with how much money he had.

11. _____ to pass the test would mean that he could not go
    to college.

12. The enemy had plans to cross the border and _____ at
    dawn.

13. Although he hated the water, he _____ himself to learn
    how to swim.

14. The story _____ what happens when there is a conflict between two kinds of duty.

Signal Words

as   **as** can signal that two things occur or develop during the same period of time.

➠ *Example*

As children get older, they grow taller.

Both of the above events occur during the same time period.

As is attached to the clause that is the reason or stimulus for the event in the other clause.

However, *as* people traveled more, they learned more and thought more about what they learned.

People traveled more is the reason that they learned more.

Look at the following sentences and decide which clause should begin with **as**. Then write the two clauses as one sentence with **as**.

➠ *Example*

    a. Winter approaches.
    b. The weather gets colder.

The approach of winter is the reason that the weather gets colder, so we can make one sentence out of **a** and **b** as follows:

As winter approaches, the weather gets colder.

1. The soccer game progressed satisfactorily for our team.

    The fans cheered louder and louder.

2. I learned to read English better.

The semester continued.

_____

3. The stars' density becomes greater and greater.

It becomes more and more difficult for anything to escape from them.

_____

4. The sound of the whistle would be high pitched.

The train approached.

_____

as   **as** can also be used instead of **because**.

▶ *Example*

As it was very cold outside, we wore warm coats.

a. Because it was very cold outside, we wore warm coats.
b. Why did we wear warm coats? Because it was very cold outside.

Both sentences have the same meaning.

As Japan was somewhat crowded with *samurai* at this time, Chikamatsu would not have had much opportunity for success in trying to have a career as a *samurai*.

Why wouldn't Chikamatsu have had much opportunity for success in trying to have a career as a *samurai*?

_____

Read the following sentences and decide if **as** is being used to signal events happening during the same time period (ST) or if it is being used as a substitute for **because** (Bec). Write **ST** or **Bec** on the blank line in front of each sentence.

_____ 1. As she walked through the garden, she picked some flowers.

_____ 2. The baby could not talk yet as she was only six months
old.

_____ 3. As it wasn't our garden, we did not pick any flowers.

_____ 4. The baby will learn to talk as she gets older.

so . . .that   **so . . . that** signals a cause and a result. The clause that
contains the word **so** is the cause. The clause that follows
the word **that** is the result.

⟶ *Example*

It is so hot that you can fry an egg on the sidewalk.

Cause: It is very hot.
Result: You can fry an egg on the sidewalk.

Read the following sentences and answer the questions:

1. I was so tired last night that I went to bed at 8:00.

   Cause: _____

   Result: _____

2. It was so cold this morning that my car would not start.

   Why wouldn't my car start?

   _____

3. The play was so successful that it saved the theater where it was
performed from bankruptcy.

   Why did the play save the theater where it was performed from bankruptcy?

   _____

4. At this time, there was a craze for love suicides, mutual suicides of a man and a woman whose plans for a life together had been so frustrated that life did not seem worth living.

When a man and a woman's plans for a life together were very frustrated, what was the result?

_____

5. The matter of black holes is so extremely dense that even light cannot escape.

What is the result of the matter of black holes being so extremely dense?

_____

Restatement

Restatement means saying the same thing in a different way.

Below are some sentences and groups of sentences. Under each one there are two more sentences marked **a** and **b**. Put a check mark (✔) in front of the sentence that is the best restatement of the original.

⟶ *Example*

People have to learn the cultural ways of their communities. They are not something that the people in the group are born with. Instinctive behavior, on the other hand, is a pattern of behavior that an animal is born with.

_____ a. People are not born knowing the cultural ways of their society but must learn them.

_____ b. Instinctive behavior does not have to be learned, but people must learn how to behave in ways that are appropriate for their culture.

The correct answer is **b**. Sentence **a** does not include the information about instinctive behavior. Put a check mark on the blank line in front of sentence **b**.

Now do the following:

1. Some people in Africa think that African termites make a delicious meal. Many other people would probably be sick if they had to eat termites, but one hundred grams of termites contain more than twice as many calories and almost twice as much protein as one hundred grams of hamburger.

_____ a. Although many people think that termites are disgusting, they are nutritious.

_____ b. Some people like to eat termites, but many people think that they are disgusting.

2. The brain of a human being is only a small part of the human body, but it is an extremely important one.

_____ a. The human brain is small and very important.

_____ b. The human brain is a very important part of the body although it is not a big part.

3. Someone with Broca's aphasia has great difficulty speaking but is able to understand speech and read and write without difficulty.

_____ a. Someone with Broca's aphasia can speak, comprehend speech, read, and write, but not very well.

_____ b. Broca's aphasia impairs people's ability to speak although it does not harm their ability to comprehend speech or to read or write.

4. Hindus and Buddhists believe that we have a succession of different lives. Each life is spent in a different body. This belief in a succession of lives in different bodies is often called reincarnation or rebirth.

_____ a. Believers in reincarnation or rebirth believe that they will have a succession of lives and that each life will be lived in a different body.

_____ b. Believers in Hinduism and Buddhism believe in reincarnation or rebirth.

5. Although it would seem that an orphan has no obligations to filial piety, this is not so. To care for one's moral nature is a filial obligation whether our parents are living or dead.

_____ a. A person who has no parents still has a filial duty to care for his moral nature.

_____ b. If a person's parents are dead, that person has no more filial duties, although he should always take of his moral nature.

6. Many people think that Europeans' belief in divine law led to a belief in natural law and that this was the reason that science orginated in Europe.

_____ a. The Europeans' belief in divine law resulted in their belief in natural law.

_____ b. It is possible that science began in Europe because Europeans believed in divine law and, as a result, could believe in natural law.

7. Today we know that our galaxy, the Milky Way, is just one of a vast number of star systems that are scattered through space.

_____ a. We now know that the Milky Way is a star system in the vast regions of space.

_____ b. We now know that there are a tremendous number of star systems in space, of which the Milky Way is only one.

8. Stars release tremendously large amounts of energy. It is for this reason that they are visible at great distances — billions of billions of miles and more.

_____ a. We can see stars that are billions of miles away from us because of the vast energy that stars release.

_____ b. We can see for billions of miles because of the energy that stars release.

9. We do not know which one of these three possibilities will happen because the answer lies in the density of the universe, which we do not know accurately enough.

_____ a. We do not know which possibility will occur because we do not know the density of the universe accurately, and we need to know it in order to predict which possibility is likely.

_____ b. There are three possibilities, and we do not know the answer as we do not know the density of the universe.

10. Although the Japanese had a strong sense of obligation to their parents and society, they also had a strong desire for human happiness.

_____ a. The Japanese had a conflict between their duty and their happiness as humans.

_____ b. The Japanese believed in their duty to their parents and their society, but they also wanted to be happy in their lives.

Comprehension Questions

Answer the following questions by circling **True** or **False** or the letter of the correct answer, or by writing the answer on the blank lines. If a statement is false, explain why it is false.

Paragraph 2

1. **True** or **False**   People are still writing *No* plays.

Paragraph 3

2. In line 6, what does "one" substitute for?

_____

Paragraph 4

3. In 1683, what was quite successful?

_____

Paragraph 5

4. True or **False**   Most of Chikamatsu's *joruri* plays were based on incidents that happened before he was born.

5. True or **False**   The idea of love suicides may have been reinforced by the popular religious belief that lovers who died together would be born together in Paradise.

6. True or **False**   *The Love Suicides of Sonezaki* was a very successful play.

Paragraph 6

7. What is the inference contained in the sentence "(Shakespeare too made contemporary references, which today we simply pass over.)"?

   a. Shakespeare made contemporary references.
   b. Shakespeare's plays have lasted until the present day and are still interesting to read.
   c. We pass over the contemporary references in Shakespeare.

Paragraph 7

8. True or **False**   People sometimes committed suicide when the conflict between obligation or duty and human happiness made happiness seem impossible.

Paragraph 8

9. True or **False**   *Chusingara* or the *Treasury of Loyal Retainers* was written by Chikamatsu.

10. True or **False**   The forty-seven *ronin* immediately killed the nobleman who caused their master to commit suicide.

11. True or **False**   The forty-seven *ronin* committed suicide because they had committed a crime when they killed the nobleman.

Paragraph 9

12. True or **False** When the forty-seven *ronin* killed the nobleman, it was an act of private vengeance.

✍ Writing Assignment

The writing assignment for this chapter and the next two chapters is the same. Write about a famous author from your country who has been dead for at least 100 years but is still famous.

Choose the person that you want to write about and begin by making short notes about his or her life. Do not write complete sentences yet. At first you just want to write down any ideas or information you have in the order in which they occur to you.

Below are some things you should include:

- Name
- Born – died
- Where he/she lived
- Titles and information about the writings of this person
- Personal life if any facts are known — married, children, and so on.
- Why is this person still famous?
- What have you read by this writer?
- Did you like it or dislike it? Why?

How can you find out the information that you do not know? Find out as much as you can by the time you finish Chapter 14. Save all your notes.

Although only twelve of her poems were published during
her lifetime, Emily Dickinson is considered one of the
greatest woman poets ever.

14 | Emily Dickinson

PRE-READING DISCUSSION

In small groups, discuss the following:

- Do you like to read poetry? (If not, why not?)
- Do you have a favorite poet? Who?
- Is this person still living?
- Why do you like this person's poetry?

The Reading Selection in this chapter is about an American poet who died over 100 years ago but is still famous. On the next page is one of her poems from the Reading Selection.

I'm Nobody!   Who are you?
Are you — Nobody — Too?
Then there's a pair of us?
Don't tell!   They'd advertise — you know!

How dreary — to be — Somebody!
How public — like a Frog —
To tell one's name — the livelong June —
To an admiring Bog!

(The words "the livelong June" mean all during the month of June.
A bog is a wet area where frogs might live.)

- Does this poem tell you anything about the author?
- What kind of person do you think she was?
- Think about her character while you read the Reading Selection.
  After you finish reading discuss her character again. Are your ideas
  about her different now or are they the same?

READING SELECTION

Emily Dickinson

E mily Dickinson was a nineteenth-century American woman who lived her life completely unknown to anyone except her family and a few friends. Less than a dozen of her poems were published during her lifetime. In spite of this, she is regarded today as a great poet, perhaps the greatest poet the United States has produced. Along with the Greek poet Sappho, she may be one of the two greatest woman poets who have ever lived.

(2)   Dickinson was born on December 10, 1830, in a small Massachusetts town called Amherst. Hers was an old family; her ancestors had come to the United States 200 years before. Her parents were not really rich, but they were certainly not poor. She had an older brother, Austin, and a younger sister, Lavinia. Her parents seem to have been rather withdrawn people, and the members of the family spent a good deal of time by themselves. She doesn't seem to have liked her mother very much. She spoke once of never really having a mother.

(3)   She was educated at the local Amherst Academy and Mount Holyoke Women's Seminary. Although she was sometimes described as pretty, she never married. In all outward respects, her life appeared to be rather boring.

(4)   The time and place in which she lived was not a good one for a woman artist to succeed. Women were expected to be obedient to men and to remain in their place at home. Rather than waste her life in the meaningless round of social events that were open to women, she decided at some point to retreat from the world in order to write her poetry. From then on, she spent a great deal of time in her bedroom writing. In later years when she was standing in front of her bedroom door, she looked at her niece and said, "It's just a turn — and freedom, Mary!" It was when she closed the door of her room and turned the key that locked the door that the most important and creative hours of her life were spent, the hours when she wrote her poetry. She was regarded as a recluse by many of her neighbors, that is, as a person who spent a good deal of time by herself.

(5)   She was actually rather proud of the fact that no one knew her. One of her poems expresses this nicely:

> I'm Nobody!   Who are you?
> Are you — Nobody — Too?
> Then there's a pair of us?
> Don't tell!   They'd advertise — you know!
>
> How dreary — to be — Somebody!
> How public — like a Frog —
> To tell one's name — the livelong June —
> To an admiring Bog!

(The use of many dashes and capitalized words is part of her style of writing.)

(6)   She showed signs of being a gifted writer rather early. Once in her teens, when her brother Austin was praised for a poem he had written, she was annoyed, feeling she could have done better. She also showed independence of spirit and a lack of respect for the male authority that dominated at this time. When her father complained that he was always given a chipped plate at meals, she took the plate to the garden and smashed it against a stone. As she put it, she did it to "remind" herself not to give her father the chipped plate again! Her youth seems to have been an active one, and there has been much speculation about a possible romantic involvement with a man. Although many historians have investigated this very carefully, no real evidence of a romance has been found.

(7)   Although she was not religious in the ordinary sense, many of her poems were concerned with God or with death. As she was isolated from most people, it probably would have made her happy if she could have felt that she was in close touch with God. Unfortunately, she seems to have felt that God kept himself hidden from her. One of her poems begins:

> I know that He exists.
> Somewhere — in Silence —
> He has hid his rare life
> From our gross eyes.

(8)   Death was an important part of her life, as it was for most people of her time. She nursed her mother for a number of years before her mother died. In her later years she had a romance with an older gentleman, Phillips Lord. Many letters were exchanged between them, but they never married, and Lord died shortly after Emily's mother did. Emily herself died not long afterwards, on May 15, 1886.

(9)   It is not known whether Emily Dickinson regarded herself as a success or failure at the time she died. Certainly, she had achieved little in the way of fame as a poet. On the other hand, she obviously had a great deal of confidence in her ability to write poetry or she would never have devoted her life to her poetry in the way that she did. There is no doubt that she wanted very much to succeed as a poet. One of her best-known poems goes as follows:

> Success is counted sweetest
> By those who ne'er succeed.
> To comprehend a nectar
> Requires sorest need.
>
> Not one of all the purple Host
> Who took the Flag today
> Can tell the definition
> So clear of Victory
>
> As he defeated — dying —
> On whose forbidden ear
> The distant strains of triumph
> Burst agonized and clear!

Interpretation of the Last Poem

Poetry can be difficult to understand even in one's native language. Understanding poetry in another language can be even more difficult and sometimes impossible. Yet the ideas expressed by great poets are universal and meaningful to all of us. Because of this, the following interpretation of the last poem in the reading selection is offered.

In the first verse, the word "nectar" refers to a sweet liquid that is found in a flower. "Sorest" means strongest or most intense. The whole verse means something like this:

> *Those who never succeed place a very high value on success. To understand something as sweet as success, one must have a strong need for it.*

In the second verse, "purple" is the color that emperors wear, and a "host" is a large group of people or an army. "Taking the flag" means winning the battle. In the third verse, "strains" refers to music; "strains of triumph" are the music of the victorious army. The ear is "forbidden" because the dying man who has lost the battle should not be hearing this victorious music. "Agonized" means painful. The second and third verses mean something like:

> *No one in the imperial army who won the battle today knows as much about victory as the dying man who has lost the battle and who hears in the distance the music of the victorious army.*

How much more beautiful the poem is than this explanation!

EXERCISES

Scanning Questions

Look back at the reading selection to find the answers to the following questions:

Paragraph 1

1. How did Emily Dickinson live her life?

   _____

2. Who is the other woman poet mentioned in this paragraph?

   _____

Paragraph 2

3. When and where was Emily Dickinson born?

   _____

Paragraph 4

4. What was expected of women in Emily Dickinson's time?

   _____

5. Why did Emily Dickinson decide to retreat from the world?

   _____

6. Where did Emily go to write her poetry?

   _____

7. What is a recluse?

   _____

Paragraph 5

8. What was she rather proud of?

_____

Paragraph 6

9. What did Emily show a lack of respect for?

_____

Paragraph 7

10. What were many of her poems concerned with?

_____

11. Why would it probably have made her happy if she could have felt in close touch with God?

_____

Paragraph 8

12. What was an important part of life for most of the people of Emily Dickinson's time?

_____

13. How old was Emily when she died?

_____

Paragraph 9

14. How much in the way of fame as a poet had Emily achieved when she died?

_____

15. What did she have a great deal of confidence in?

_____

Vocabulary

Fill in the blanks with the correct words from the list below. Sentence **a** of each pair is from the reading selection. Sentence **b** of each pair uses the same word as sentence **a** with the same meaning.

> annoy(ed)   gifted   respects
> authority   obedient   withdrawn

1a. Her parents seem to have been rather _____ people, and the members of the family spent a good deal of time by themselves.

  b. Since his wife's death, Mr. Jones has become very

_____. He rarely goes out of his house or sees other people.

2a. In all outward _____, her life appeared to be rather boring.

  b. The furnace didn't work very efficiently, but in all other

_____, their new house seemed perfect.

3a. Women were expected to be _____ to men and to remain in their place at home.

  b. My dog is very _____. When I give her a command, she obeys it.

4a. She showed signs of being a _____ writer rather early.

  b. John can not sing very well, but he is a _____ pianist. He is one of the best pianists I have ever heard.

5a. Once in her teens, when her brother Austin was praised for a poem

he had written, she was _____, feeling that she could
have done much better.

b. While I was involved in an important phone call today, my child
kept trying to talk to me. After the third time this happened, I be-

came _____ with her and told her to leave the room.

6a. She also showed independence of spirit and a lack of respect for the

male _____ that dominated at this time.

b. Parents have _____ over their young children. They
decide on what is best for their children to do, and the children are
supposed to do what their parents tell them to do.

Do the same with the following:

complain(ed)   dominate(d)   investigate(d)
confidence   exchange(d)   romantic

7a. She also showed independence of spirit and a lack of respect for the

male authority that _____ at this time.

b. In the United States during the 1980s, the idea of being physically

healthy _____ people's thinking. They became very
concerned about what they ate and about getting plenty of exercise.
Running and jogging became popular, and many people joined
health clubs.

8a. When her father _____ that he was always given a
chipped plate at meals, she took the plate to the garden and
smashed it against a stone.

b. She _____s about everything I cook for her. She says
she does not like it, or it is too hot or too cold. She always finds
something wrong.

9a. Her youth seems to have been an active one, and there has been

much speculation about a possible _____ involvement with a man.

b. John and Mary are just good friends. There isn't anything

_____ about their relationship. They are not in love.

10a. Although many historians have _____ this very carefully, no real evidence of a romance has been found.

b. The police _____ the robbery, and after a while, they
caught the robber.

11a. Many letters were _____ between them, but they
never married.

b. We _____ gifts with friends and relatives at
Christmas.

12a. On the other hand, she obviously had a great deal of

_____ in her ability to write poetry.

b. John had _____ in himself. He knew he was a good
athlete, and he expected to win the race.

Self-Test

Fill in the blanks with the correct words from the list below.

annoys	complain	dominates	gifted	obedient
authority	confidence	exchange	investigated	

1. The weatherman has predicted a nice day, but I don't have much

_____ in his prediction. It is getting colder and cloudy.

2. The people in the next apartment play music too loudly. It

   _____ me.

3. When I _____ to them about the loud music, they stop for a while, but in a day or two, it gets loud again.

4. He is not an _____ little boy. He does not do what his parents tell him to do.

5. Last night, I heard a loud noise downstairs. When I

   _____ it, I discovered that the cat had knocked a pile of books off the table.

6. Nowadays it is customary to _____ business cards when you meet other business people.

7. Some children are academically _____. They learn very rapidly in school.

8. When the weather gets very cold, it _____ our activities. No one wants to do things outside when the temperature is –20°F.

9. Police officers have the _____ to arrest people.

Prediction: Signal Words

Circle the letter of the answer that will best complete each of the following according to the signal word.

1. I walked so many miles yesterday that

   a. is why my legs are still very tired today.
   b. my legs are still very tired today.
   c. it was ten miles.

2. Stars are visible at great distances because

   a. we can see them.
   b. we cannot see some stars called *black holes*.
   c. they release tremendously large amounts of energy.

3. I can't go to the movies with you tonight. However,

   a. I can go tomorrow if you want to.
   b. I have to study.
   c. I can't go tomorrow, either.

4. I can't go to the movies with you tonight as

   a. I can go tomorrow.
   b. I have to study for a test.
   c. you are going to the movies tonight.

5. Not all stars become white dwarfs. For example,

   a. some stars continue to shrink until they become neutron stars.
   b. white dwarfs do not shine any more.
   c. our sun is part of the Milky Way galaxy.

6. John is very busy this summer. For one thing, he is taking three courses in summer school. In addition,

   a. he will graduate in December.
   b. he is working twenty hours a week.
   c. his courses are interesting.

7. The novels of some authors are based on their own lives, such as

   a. Chikamatsu lived in Japan.
   b. Charles Dickens visited the United States.
   c. Charles Dickens' novel *David Copperfield*.

8. Mary passed the language exam, so

   a. John did not.
   b. she was able to graduate.
   c. it was a difficult exam.

9. Chikamatsu wrote plays for the puppet theater. He also

    a. wrote plays for the Kabuki theater.
    b. was enormously successful.
    c. was born to *samurai* parents.

10. Mary passed the language exam, but

    a. she was able to graduate.
    b. John did not.
    c. John did, too.

Words with More Than One Meaning

Study each set of sentences below. Sentence **a** of each set is from the vocabulary exercises in Chapters 9 through 14. Sentence **b** and sentence **c** of each set use the same word with two different meanings. Below each set of sentences are three meanings. Write the letter of the appropriate sentence in front of each meaning.

1a. Stars release tremendous <u>amounts</u> of energy.
  b. The <u>amount</u> of the hotel bill plus meals was $125.00.
  c. What he says is not true. It <u>amounts</u> to a lie.

   _____   is the same as
   _____   quantities
   _____   total

2a. Aristotle developed a picture of the universe in which the earth was the <u>center</u> of everything.
  b. The distance from the edge of a circle to the <u>center</u> of the circle is called the radius.
  c. The author was the <u>center</u> of everyone's interest at the party.

   _____   middle
   _____   point around which everything else revolves
   _____   main object of attention

3a. Chikamatsu's play <u>concerned</u> the love of a shop clerk and the woman he wanted to marry.
b. When she did not come home at the usual time, her parents became <u>concerned</u> about her.
c. Their new store was a successful <u>concern</u>.

_____ business
_____ worried
_____ was about

4a. The opposite of expand is <u>contract</u>.
b. In English we usually <u>contract</u> pairs of words such as **can** plus **not** into **can't**.
c. The movie actor signed a <u>contract</u> for his next movie.

_____ become smaller
_____ make shorter by omitting something
_____ a legal agreement

5a. Deep inside the earth, there is a dense <u>core</u> made of iron and nickel.
b. The <u>core</u> of our problem is that we do not have enough money. If we had enough money, we could solve some of our other problems.
c. Most people do not eat the <u>core</u> of an apple.

_____ most important or basic part
_____ the hard central part with the seeds
_____ the central part of the earth

6a. The salary that a teacher receives is <u>determined</u> by the number of years he or she has taught.
b. He is <u>determined</u> to win this game.
c. They looked at all the stolen TV sets that the police had found and <u>determined</u> which one was theirs.

_____ identified from several
_____ will not let anything prevent him
_____ related to, caused by

7a. Stars three times the mass of the sun will <u>exhaust</u> their hydrogen in half a billion years.
  b. I was <u>exhausted</u> after running ten miles.
  c. The matter in the <u>exhaust</u> from a car can cause air pollution.

_____ waste material from an engine
_____ use up
_____ extremely tired

8a. He tried to <u>extend</u> his arm upward until his hand touched the ceiling, but he was not tall enough.
  b. She <u>extended</u> herself as much as she could, but she did not win the race.
  c. The professor said my composition was too short. He wanted me to <u>extend</u> it.

_____ try harder than normal
_____ make longer
_____ stretch to fullest length

9a. The sun was also extremely important to them, and it was even more <u>regular</u> in its movements than the Nile.
  b. It was a <u>regular</u> day at work. Nothing unusual happened.
  c. They were <u>regular</u> customers of that restaurant. They ate there about once a week.

_____ ordered, unchanging
_____ doing the same thing often
_____ ordinary, usual

10a. The core that <u>remains</u> behind after the explosion is very small.
  b. The weather <u>remained</u> hot all week.
  c. A cure for cancer <u>remains</u> to be found.

_____ is left behind
_____ still needs to be developed or solved
_____ continues unchanged

Comprehension Questions

Answer the following questions by circling **True** or **False** or the letter of the correct answer, or by writing your answer on the blank lines. If a statement is false, explain why it is false.

Paragraph 1

1. In lines 4 and 5, the words "In spite of this" signal a contrast. What is the contrast?

   a. She wasn't well known in her own lifetime but is regarded as a great poet now.

   b. She lived her life completely unknown to anyone except family and a few friends, but she published less than a dozen poems in her lifetime.

   c. Neither **a** nor **b**.

Paragraph 2

2. "She doesn't seem to have liked her mother very much."

   There is a sentence in this paragraph that gives a specific detail about the above sentence. What is it?

   _____

Paragraph 4

3. Why was the time and place in which she lived not a good one for a woman artist to succeed?

   _____

4. Why did Emily regard being locked in her room as "freedom"?

   _____

Paragraph 6

5. "She also showed ...a lack of respect for the male authority that dominated at this time."

   In this paragraph, there is a specific example of Emily showing her lack of respect for male authority. What is it?

   _____

Paragraph 7

6. **True** or **False**   Emily did not feel she was in close touch with God.

7. **True** or **False**   The poem in this paragraph is an example of Emily's feeling that God hid himself from her.

Paragraph 9

8. The author thinks that Emily had a great deal of confidence in her ability to write poetry. Which of the following tells why he thinks so?

   a. At the time she died, she had achieved little fame as a poet.
   b. She achieved little fame as a poet, but she wanted very much to succeed.
   c. She achieved little fame as a poet, but she devoted her life to her poetry anyway.

✍ Writing Assignment

Write a one-paragraph summary of paragraphs 1, 2, and 3. Use the method you have used before in this book. Combine all the information in the three paragraphs into one paragraph. When you finish the summary, look at your notes about the author you have chosen to write about. Write some sentences about him or her.

"Portrait of Dostoevsky" from *The Idiot*, wood engraving, 8″ × 5″.
Courtesy of New York Public Library Collection.

15 | Fyodor Dostoevsky

In small groups, discuss the following:

- What is your favorite novel?
- Why is it your favorite?
- What are the characters in the novel like?
- Are there good people and bad people?
- Are the good people always good?
- Are the bad people always bad?
- Is the novel like real life?
- Should a novel always be like real life (except for science fiction!)?
- Should novels always end happily?

READING SELECTION

Fyodor Dostoevsky

Fyodor Dostoevsky, who was born in Russia in 1821, was one of the greatest of the Russian novelists. Indeed, he was one of the world's greatest novelists. Dostoevsky was very concerned with his characters' motives, even if they were bad ones. He tried to really understand people's motives, the reasons why they do what they do. Some nineteenth-century novelists were content to describe how their characters are different from each other. The motives of their characters tend to be rather obvious, and their characters are mostly all good or all bad. Dostoevsky's characters are more complicated, with good and bad mixed together.

(2)   Dostoevky's mother died when he was young. She was the daughter of a merchant who had lost most of his money when the French captured Moscow in 1812. She had a lifelong interest in literature and the arts that undoubtedly influenced her son.

(3)   Dostoevky's father was a doctor from the Lithuanian nobility. The name Dostoevsky comes from the word *dostoynyy*, meaning *worthy*. Dostoevky's father was melancholy and suspicious on the one hand, but energetic and resourceful on the other. He saw to it that Fyodor got an education at the Academy of Engineers in St. Petersburg. Dostoevky's father owned a piece of land that was farmed by a number of people called serfs. These serfs were actually close to what we would now call slaves; they were bought and sold with the land that they lived on. Dostoevsky's father died in 1839 in somewhat mysterious circumstances. The truth is probably that he had a stroke while shouting at a group of serfs on his property. There is a persistent rumor, however, that he was murdered by his serfs during an argument.

(4)   Dostoevsky was a writer from an early age. His first novel, *Poor Folk*, was finished in 1845. During the same period of Dostoevsky's youth when he was writing his first novels and stories, he became involved with a revolutionary group led by a man named Petrashevsky. Fyodor himself was probably not an active revolutionary, but nevertheless he was arrested in 1849. Dostoevsky tried to minimize his own participation in revolutionary activities, but he did not speak against any of the other members of the group. Along with twenty others who had been arrested at the same time, Dostoevsky was condemned to death.

(5)   Although the ruler at that time, Czar Nicholas, did not really intend to have any of these twenty-one people executed, he treated them in a very

cruel way. Until the last minute, he let all of them believe that they were to be hanged. They were taken to the execution ground and three of them had hoods put on them and were led to the scaffold. Finally, a carriage appeared at the last minute with word from the Czar that they were pardoned. By this time one of the three men that had been led to the scaffold had gone insane. This terrible experience was one that Dostoevsky never forgot.

(6) Although no longer condemned to death, Dostoevsky had to serve four years in a Siberian prison camp and remained in Siberia for a total of ten years. It was while he was in Siberia that he married his first wife, Maria. It was also in Siberia that he had his first epileptic fit. These fits were to recur throughout his life and had a great influence on him. He described the moment before the fit as one of "unthinkable joy." One of his later novels, *The Idiot*, is about a person with epilepsy and is probably based on his own experiences.

(7) Dostoevsky wrote a novel about his experiences in Siberia called *The House of the Dead*. His life after Siberia continued to be a troubled one. His first wife died of tuberculosis, but even before then he became involved in a love affair with a woman named Polina Suslova. Gambling fascinated him, and he wasted a good deal of both time and money at gambling.

(8) He found a woman who acted as his secretary, and so he began dictating his novels to her. With her help he was able to write a short novel, *The Gambler*, in only a month. This woman, Anna, became his second wife. Although his life remained deeply troubled, Anna provided a great deal of support for him with her intelligence and common sense.

(9) It was in the latter part of his life that he wrote his four greatest novels: *Crime and Punishment, The Idiot, The Possessed,* and *The Brothers Karamazov*. All his novels are at a high emotional pitch and explore negative thoughts of hatred and disgust that some other novelists of the time would not deal with. *Crime and Punishment* deals with a young man who murders an old woman for her money. *The Idiot*, as was said, deals with a person with epilepsy. *The Possessed* deals with a group of revolutionaries. His last novel, *The Brothers Karamazov*, is generally viewed as his best. It concerns a group of brothers and their murdered father. The characters of the brothers are developed in great detail. Dostoevsky died in 1881 rather suddenly of a lung disease that may have been emphysema.

(10) Throughout his life Dostoevsky was concerned with the Christian value of love. To the end of his life, he kept a copy of the New Testament that had been given to him when he left for Siberia. In his last novel, a dying priest, Father Zossima, speaks to the people around him about love, saying the famous words "Fathers and teachers, I ask you, what is hell? I maintain that it is the suffering of being unable to love."

EXERCISES

Scanning Questions

Look back at the reading selection to find the answers to the following questions:

Paragraph 1

1. Where and when was Dostoevsky born?

   _____

2. What was Dostoevsky concerned about?

   _____

3. What are *motives*?

   _____

4. Whose characters are mostly all good or all bad?

   _____

5. Whose characters are more complicated?

   _____

Paragraph 3

6. Who were bought and sold with the land they lived on?

   _____

7. This paragraph suggests two possibilities concerning the death of Dostoevsky's father. What are they?

_____

_____

Paragraph 4

8. What was the name of Dostoevsky's first novel?

_____

9. When was he arrested?

_____

10. Who were condemned to death?

_____

Paragraph 5

11. What did the Czar let the twenty-one people believe until the last minute?

_____

12. What happened at the last minute?

_____

Paragraph 6

13. How long was Dostoevsky in a Siberian prison camp?

_____

14. How long was he in Siberia?

_____

15. Which novel is probably based on his own experience as a person with epilepsy?

_____

Paragraph 7

16. What was the title of the novel about his experiences in Siberia?

_____

Paragraph 9

17. What were his four greatest novels?

_____   _____

_____   _____

18. What kind of thoughts did Dostoevsky's novels explore?

_____

19. Which novel is generally viewed as his best?

_____

20. When did Dostoevsky die?

_____

Vocabulary

Fill in the blanks with the correct words from the list below. Sentence **a** of each pair of sentences is from the reading selection. Sentence **b** of each pair uses the same word as sentence **a** with the same meaning.

circumstances   resourceful   worthy
persistent   suspicious

1a. The name Dostoevsky comes from the word *dostoynyy*, meaning

_____.

b. He had done well, and I thought he was _____ of being promoted.

2a. Dostoevsky's father was melancholy and _____ on
the one hand, but energetic and resourceful on the other.

b. The detective was _____ of the red-haired man. He
believed that that man had committed the murder.

3a. Dostoevsky's father was melancholy and suspicious on the one

hand, but energetic and _____ on the other.

b. She was very _____. She knew just what to do in an
emergency.

4a. Dostoevsky's father died in 1839 in somewhat mysterious

_____.

b. The policeman tried to find out the _____ of the accident. He needed to know exactly how it had happened.

5a. There is a _____ rumor, however, that he was murdered by his serfs during an argument.

b. He was a very _____ salesman. It was very difficult to get rid of him.

Do the same with the following:

intend	participation	support
maintain(ed)	recur	waste(d)

6a. Dostoevsky tried to minimize his own _____ in revolutionary activities, but he did not speak against any of the other members of the group.

b. She was very active in helping the children in the after-school programs. At the end of the year, they all thanked her for her

_____ in their activities.

7a. Although the ruler at that time, Czar Nicholas, did not really

_____ to have any of these twenty-one people executed, he treated them in a very cruel way.

b. I _____ to go home and go to bed when this is over. I am very tired.

8a. These fits were to _____ throughout his life and had a great influence on him.

b. When I spilled the ink all over my desk, the teacher told me to be

sure that an accident like this did not _____. Since then I have been very careful so that it wouldn't happen again.

9a. Gambling fascinated him, and he _____ a good deal of both time and money at gambling.

b. I consider the time I spent in that class to be completely

_____. I didn't learn a thing.

10a. Although his life remained deeply troubled, Anna provided a great deal of _____ for him with her intelligence and common sense.

  b. He gave me a lot of _____ when my mother died. He was always ready to listen to me and help me out.

11a. "I _____ that it is the suffering of being unable to love."

  b. He _____ that he was innocent of the crime, but no one believed him.

Self-Test

Fill in the blanks with the correct words from the list below.

circumstances	persistent	support
intend	recur	suspicious
participation	resourceful	wasted

1. He was a very _____ person. He thought almost everyone was trying to injure him.

2. Please come to the meeting on Friday. Your _____ will be greatly appreciated.

3. She was very sad, so I tried to cheer her up. I felt she needed my

_____.

4. The _____ of the accident were such that I felt he was not to blame.

5. I hope Saturday is sunny because I _____ to go the beach if the weather is nice.

6. I'm sorry I _____ my money on that dress. It doesn't look good on me at all.

7. My headaches tend to _____ every third or fourth day. I wish they didn't come again so often.

8. He showed himself to be very _____. He was able to get out of trouble without help.

9. I have a very _____ headache. It doesn't go away when I take aspirin.

Word Families

In the list below, there are different forms of some of the vocabulary words in Chapters 13, 14, and 15. The new forms are different parts of speech.
Study the words below before you do the exercise.

Verbs	Nouns	Adjectives	Adverbs
intend	intention	——	——
fail	failure	failed/failing	——
persist	persistence	persistent	persistently
succeed	success	successful	successfully
waste	waste	wasteful	wastefully

1. intend   intention

  a. It is my _____ to go to medical school after I graduate.

  b. I _____ to take two classes in summer school so I can graduate next year.

2. fail   failure   failed/failing

  a. I hope I can pass this class. I hope that I don't

     _____ it.

  b. The student received a _____ grade in the exam.

c. I had to walk up six flights of stairs because of the

_____ of the elevator to work.

d. Our plan didn't succeed. Because of our _____ plan,
we lost the game.

3. persist   persistence   persistent

a. It is not easy to learn another language, but if you

_____, you will eventually learn it.

b. We wanted to have a picnic in our backyard, but the mosquitos

kept biting us. They were so _____ that we finally
went in the house.

c. John failed some courses, but he kept studying and finally gradu-

ated. His _____ helped him to graduate.

4. succeed   success   successful

a. John was finally _____ because he persisted.

b. There is an old saying that "if at first you don't

_____, try, try again."

c. John's _____ was achieved by hard work.

5. waste   waste   wasteful   wastefully

a. It is better to plan how you are going to spend your money. If you

don't, you will just _____ it.

b. You should not spend your money _____. If you do,
you will not have money for the things that you need.

   c. Americans produce a great deal of garbage. Soon there will not be

   any places to put all this _____.

   d. Throwing away leftover food is _____. It can be
   warmed and eaten the next day.

Synonyms

Write a synonym for the underlined word or words in the sentences below. There may be more
than one possible synonym for some words. Use your dictionary to help you if necessary.

   1. When you let the air out of a balloon, it <u>gets smaller</u>.

   _____

   2. Parents have an <u>obligation</u> to their children.

   _____

   3. We had a large <u>amount</u> of snow last winter.

   _____

   4. Something unusual <u>happened</u> at work yesterday.

   _____

   5. There is a dot in the <u>middle</u> of this circle. (•)

   _____

   6. The average of your test grades and your homework <u>determines</u> your
   final grade.

   _____

   7. My opinion is <u>contrary</u> to yours.

   _____

8. You must give your plants an <u>adequate amount</u> of water but not too much water.

_____

Antonyms

Rewrite each sentence below using an antonym for each of the underlined words. Be sure that the sentence makes sense. Use your dictionary to help you if necessary.

1. The coffee pot is <u>full</u>.

_____

2. It may <u>continue</u> raining tonight.

_____

3. This is a <u>temporary</u> home for us. We are planning to move soon.

_____

4. Those two patterns are <u>the same</u>.

_____

5. I am <u>not sure</u> that John is home.

_____

6. John was a <u>failure</u> in his last job.

_____

7. She is always <u>early</u>.

_____

8. Mary <u>lacks</u> a sense of humor. She doesn't laugh very much.

Literal and Figurative Meanings

Many words and expressions can be used with both a *literal* (real) meaning and with what is called a *figurative* meaning. For example, the literal meaning of the verb *carry* is to transport something while you are holding it in your arms.

> **a.** Mary is carrying a bag of groceries.

However, we can also use carry with a figurative meaning.

> **b.** Mary is carrying a full load of courses at the university this summer.

In sentence **a**, the literal meaning, Mary is actually holding a bag of groceries in her arms.

In sentence **b**, the figurative meaning, Mary is not holding her courses in her arms. In fact, they are not things that can be held in your arms. Therefore, sentence **b** is using the word "carry" with a figurative meaning.

Read each pair of sentences below. Decide which sentence uses the underlined word with a literal (**L**) meaning and which one uses the word with a figurative (**F**) meaning. Write **L** or **F** on the blank lines.

⟱ *Example*

    L   **a.** I <u>walked</u> to work.
    F   **b.** The instructor <u>walked</u> us through the difficult reading, paragraph by paragraph.

In sentence **a**, <u>walked</u> means the physical act of walking, so it is the literal meaning.

Sentence **b** means that the instructor helped us to understand the reading by carefully explaining it to us as we read it. This is a figurative meaning.

1. _____ a. Paper towels <u>absorb</u> water.
   _____ b. John <u>absorbs</u> new ideas rapidly.

2. _____ a. During my travels, I <u>accumulated</u> a great deal of new knowledge about the rest of the world.
   _____ b. Mary <u>accumulated</u> a large library because she bought several new books every week.

3. _____ a. She <u>attracts</u> many friends because she is such a nice person.
   _____ b. A magnet <u>attracts</u> iron.

4. _____ a. That plan <u>contains</u> many problems.
   _____ b. A glass can <u>contain</u> water.

5. _____ a. There were a lot of people in the room. It was very <u>crowded</u>.
   _____ b. When I thought about the problem, ideas began to <u>crowd</u> into my mind.

6. _____ a. If fire gets near gasoline, there will be an <u>explosion</u>.
   _____ b. Ten years ago, there weren't many books about this subject. However, in the past few years, there has been an <u>explosion</u> of new books about it.

7. _____ a. They <u>raised</u> the flag up the flagpole.
   _____ b. Your solution to this problem <u>raises</u> many new problems.

8. _____ a. Her life <u>revolves</u> around her home and her family.
   _____ b. The earth <u>revolves</u> around the sun.

9. _____ a. I was tired of thinking about the problem, so I <u>shifted</u> my thoughts to something else.
   _____ b. He <u>shifted</u> his books from the chair to the floor so that another student could sit there.

10. _____ a. The speech was not very good. The speaker <u>traveled</u> from one topic to another without any connections.
    _____ b. He has <u>traveled</u> to many different countries.

Comprehension Questions

Answer the following questions by circling **True** or **False** or the letter of the correct answer. If a statement is false, explain why it is false.

Paragraph 1

1. **True** or **False**   The characters in Dostoevsky's novels were more complicated than the characters in the novels of some other nineteenth-century novelists.

Paragraph 3

2. Find the word "but" in the third sentence of this paragraph. "But" signals a contrast here. What is the contrast?

   a. between Dostoevsky's father and Dostoevsky
   b. between four characteristics of Dostoevsky's father
   c. between two unpleasant characteristics and two good characteristics of Dostoevsky's father

3. **True** or **False**   We definitely know how Dostoevsky's father died.

Paragraph 4

4. **True** or **False**   Dostoevsky was arrested because he was an active revolutionary.

Paragraph 5

5. **True** or **False**   The Czar planned to execute the twenty-one men, but he changed his mind.

Paragraph 6

6. **True** or **False**   Dostoevsky left Siberia when he got out of prison.

Paragraph 7

7. **True** or **False**   The third and fourth sentences of this paragraph are examples of Dostoevsky's troubled life after Siberia.

Paragraph 8

8. True or **False**   Dostoevsky finished *The Gambler* quickly because he had a secretary to write what he was
saying.

Paragraph 9

9. True or **False**   There were some nineteenth-century novelists
who did not want to deal with negative thoughts
of hatred and disgust in their novels.

Paragraph 10

10. True or **False**   We can infer that the New Testament probably includes writing about the Christian value of love.

✐ Writing Assignment

Look at the sentences you wrote about your author after Chapter 14. Do you want to add anything? Do you want to change any sentences? Do you want to write your sentences in a different order? Are all the sentences grammatically correct?

When you finish making your changes and corrections, rewrite your sentences on a new piece of paper in the form of a paragraph.